DARK JOURNEY DEEP GRACE

God bless you on your journey
into deep grace

Roy Ratcliff

JEFFREY DAHMER'S STORY OF FAITH

DARK JOURNEY DEEP GRACE

ROY RATCLIFF WITH LINDY ADAMS

LEAFWOOD
PUBLISHERS

ACKNOWLEDGEMENTS

I would like to thank my wife, Susan, and my daughter, Manda, for badgering me to write this book. As Susan said, the story needed to be told beyond Jeff's death. I would also like to thank Donna Fox and Glenda Conrad for their encouragement to write this book. I would like to thank Bryan Koontz for his wise counsel and advice, and Teresa Dunlap for her initial editing that helped me formulate my thoughts.

ROY RATCLIFF

Dark Journey, Deep Grace
Jeffrey Dahmer's Journey of Faith
Published by Leafwood Publishers

Copyright 2006 by Roy Ratcliff

ISBN 0-9767790-2-1
Printed in the United States of America

Book design by Greg Jackson, Thinkpen Design

For information contact:
Leafwood Publishers, Abilene, Texas
1-877-816-4455 toll free
www.leafwoodpublishers.com

06 07 08 09 10 11 12 13 14 / 10 9 8 7 6 5 4 3 2 1

THE CHIEF OF SINNERS

BY ROB MCRAY

This article was published in 1994 in *Wineskins* magazine before Jeffrey Dahmer's death.
At that time, Rob McRay was minister of the Northtown Church, Milwaukee, Wisconsin.
Today McRay is the minister of the Donelson Church of Christ, Nashville, Tennessee.
Copyright *Wineskins* magazine, Vol. 2, No. 6, 1994. Reprinted by permission.

"WHO do you think are candidates for the title, 'the chief of sinners'?"
We were studying I Timothy in our Wednesday Bible study. Our text was
Paul's description of himself as a violent, blasphemous persecutor who had
been saved by grace. My question was slow to draw response. One theologi-
cally astute member responded that he was—that each of us is as guilty of
being a sinner as anyone else. He made a valid point. But Paul seemed to be
saying that as the chief of sinners, he was somehow worse than the rank and
file of sinners. So I pressed on, and the nominations were those I expected.

After Hitler, I knew that in Milwaukee Jeffrey Dahmer would be among the first nominated—and he was.

Jeffrey Dahmer is our local monster. He is serving 15 consecutive life sentences in a Wisconsin prison for 17 of the most grotesque murders ever committed. His crimes are so unimaginably horrifying that I cannot even describe them. In Milwaukee you don't have to—they were vividly described, day after day, in graphic detail, during his televised trial.

Was Paul really a worse sinner than Dahmer? If God's unlimited mercy could save Paul, could it also save Dahmer? The question prompted an interesting and, for most of us, unsettling theoretical discussion. The one who seemed the most comfortable that Dahmer could also be saved by God's grace was the member who had identified himself as the chief of sinners.

Late Wednesday afternoon, April 6—just four weeks after that class—I found myself on the phone with Curtis Booth, who said he worked with a prison ministry in Oklahoma. A prisoner in Wisconsin had completed a Bible correspondence course and wanted to be baptized. They needed a local minister to arrange it. We had talked for several minutes before he mentioned the prisoner's name...Jeffrey Dahmer.

I admit I was speechless. The thought occurred to me that I had been made the object of some kind of prank. I finally, hesitatingly, asked, "Is this legit?" Booth's response was, "Yes. Do you know who Jeffrey Dahmer is?" I assured him that everyone in Milwaukee knew who Dahmer was.

His story seemed somehow credible and incredible at the same time. Mary Mott, a Christian in Virginia, had seen a television report on Jeffrey Dahmer and concluded that if anyone needed the gospel, he did. And so she sent him a Bible correspondence course. Jeffrey Dahmer was searching for some answer to the distress in his conscience (surely that must be an understatement). The Bible study offered a glimmer of hope.

I explained to Curtis Booth that the prison was a few hours away, that I was leaving the next morning for a theology conference, but that I would find someone to take care of it. I then called the prison chaplain to try to confirm the story, but he had left for the day. Still uncertain that the story could be true, and reeling from the implications if it were, I called Roy Ratcliff. Roy is a minister in Madison, Wisconsin, a friend I felt I could call, and a man who knows the gospel of grace. I related the story, confessed my confusion, offered my assistance and left town.

The chaplain told Roy that Dahmer had indeed requested to be baptized. He agreed to set up a meeting and to investigate where the baptism could be performed. A couple of weeks later Roy sat in a small room inside the prison and waited uneasily for Jeffrey Dahmer to enter. Roy discovered that Jeffrey was as anxious about the meeting as he was.

Jeffrey's biggest fear was that Roy would say "No"—that Roy would tell him he could not be baptized. When Roy said that he would indeed baptize Jeffrey, and that he would come back regularly to study with him, Jeffrey seemed genuinely amazed, relieved and grateful.

On Tuesday, May 10, in a whirlpool in the Columbia Correctional Institution, Roy baptized Jeffrey Dahmer in the name of Jesus Christ.

Earlier that same day John Wayne Gacy was executed in Illinois. But Wisconsin doesn't have the death penalty, so Jeffrey will spend the rest of his life in prison. And there is nothing he can ever do to atone for his crimes. He will die in prison and there is nothing...nothing he can do to atone for his sins.

But the blood of Jesus Christ can cleanse even "the chief of sinners!" If it can't—if Jeffrey Dahmer cannot be saved by grace—then no one can. Not me...and not you.

> *Here is a trustworthy saying that deserves full acceptance: Christ Jesus came into the world to save sinners—of whom I am the worst. But for that very reason I was shown mercy so that in me, the worst of sinners, Christ Jesus might display his unlimited patience as an example for those who would believe on him and receive eternal life. (1 Timothy 1:15-16, NIV)*

"Jeff confessed to me his great remorse for his crimes.

He wished he could do something for the families

of his victims to make it right, but there was nothing he could do.

He turned to God because there was no one else to turn to,

but he showed great courage in his daring to ask the question,

'Is heaven for me too?' I think many people are resentful of him

for asking that question. But he dared to ask,

and he dared to believe the answer."

ROY RATCLIFF
JEFFREY DAHMER'S MEMORIAL SERVICE
DECEMBER 2, 1994

CONTENTS

FOREWORD
THE CHIEF OF SINNERS, BY ROB MCRAY   5

CHAPTER 1   THE CALL   13

CHAPTER 2   THE MEETING   23

CHAPTER 3   DARK JOURNEY   37

CHAPTER 4   WHY?   45

CHAPTER 5   FINDING FAITH   55

CHAPTER 6   THE BAPTISM   63

CHAPTER 7   THE MEDIA   75

CHAPTER 8   DEEP GRACE   87

CHAPTER 9   ATTACKED   101

CHAPTER 10   THE LETTER   113

CHAPTER 11   FRIENDSHIP   123

CHAPTER 12   JOURNEY'S END   131

CHAPTER 13   THE MEMORIAL   141

CHAPTER 14   REFLECTIONS: SANE OR INSANE?   151

CHAPTER 15   REFLECTIONS: WAS HE SINCERE?   159

EPILOGUE   I CALLED HIM JEFF   167

BIBLIOGRAPHY   175

CHAPTER 1
THE CALL

*"Lionel and Shari Dahmer requested a ten-minute private
meeting with their son before he was led away....Dahmer was
straightway taken to the Correctional Institute at Portage in upstate
Wisconsin, where the following day the director received
nearly two hundred enquiries from authors and mental health
experts wishing to interview him."*

Brian Masters
The Shrine of Jeffrey Dahmer, 1993

ON April 6, 1994, a phone call changed my life. There was nothing unusual or special about that day that would indicate something life-changing was going to happen. It was a day like so many others.

Around suppertime the call came. It was a good friend, Rob McRay, a preacher in Milwaukee. It was unusual for him to be calling me at suppertime on a Wednesday night because both of our churches have a Wednesday night service. We are usually getting ready for those responsibilities.

But this call was something quite out of the norm.

As a minister, I am accustomed to receiving phone calls at all times of the day and night. It is a defining part of the ministry of serving people. Most of the time these calls are from people who are hurting and just need someone to listen to their story as they pour their hearts out. Such interruptions are the price of being in a noble profession.

Rob had just talked with a minister in Oklahoma active in prison work, Curtis Booth, who was in contact with a prisoner here in Wisconsin who wanted to become a Christian. The prison is in Portage, Wisconsin, about 40 miles north of Madison where I live. Rob was leaving for a conference in

Chicago and knew I lived closer to the prison than he did, so he was calling to ask me to follow up. I had never done prison work, but I was willing to do what I could.

As a minister, I had given my life to God, which meant going wherever whenever he needed me. Like most ministers, I relate to the Old Testament story of Moses encountering the burning bush. The burning bush was a sign to Moses that God was calling him to lead the Israelites. Moses could not escape the call of the "I AM THAT I AM." Ministers don't always know what God intends for them—until they are called.

So I told Rob, "Sure, I'll look into it. What is the prisoner's name?"

Rob asked if I were sitting down, which piqued my curiosity. "I'm not sure if this is a hoax," he said, "because April 1st was only a few days ago. This is a little unbelievable."

He paused, then said, "The prisoner's name is Jeffrey Dahmer."

"Rob, did you say, 'Jeffrey Dahmer?'" I asked.

"That's right."

Rob had lived in Milwaukee during Jeffrey Dahmer's trial, hearing all the horrible details of his crimes. I think Rob was glad to hand the task over to me. It was a little too personal for him to handle.

He continued, "I tried to call the chaplain at the Columbia Correctional Institution to verify the story, but he had already left. I'm leaving for my conference, and I simply cannot follow through on this. Would you call to see if the request is true, and if so, follow up on it?"

Questions multiplied in my mind. What would my family think? I'd been married for 25 years to my lovely wife, Susan, and in all that time, I'd never exposed her to anything harmful. My children were grown. Would they take this matter seriously, or would they make jokes or laugh about it? Would they encourage or discourage me? What would my congregation think? I had only served them for four years, and I still didn't know them all well. Would they be honored or ashamed? Most importantly, is Dahmer sincere? Could he have a hidden motive?

Finally, I answered. "Yes, I'll call the chaplain tomorrow. If Dahmer really wants to be baptized, I'll make the arrangements." We said our goodbyes, and I hung up.

I put the phone down, turned, and told Susan and my daughter, who was with us, "You're not going to believe this. I was just asked to baptize Jeffrey Dahmer." They were stunned for a moment, but quickly recovered. It wasn't long before we began to joke around about this strange happening that came so out of the blue. We couldn't imagine the immense impact this would have on our lives.

At church that night, I told my congregation what had happened. I asked for their prayers. I said I didn't know if the story was accurate, but, yes, I had received a call asking me to baptize a prisoner in Portage, Wisconsin, and that prisoner was Jeffrey Dahmer. The eyes of some grew wide with astonishment. Some were speechless. A few came to me later and said they would pray for me.

How do you relax after a request like this one? Predictably, I had trouble getting to sleep that night. Questions floated across my mind. Was the prisoner really Jeffrey Dahmer? Did he really want to be a Christian? What would he know, or want to know, about baptism? What kind of a person is he? Was this a cruel joke? And—most importantly—why me?

I knew all these issues would seem clearer in the morning, but I knew what I had to do first. I had to confirm the truth of the request. I also decided to contact a minister closer to the prison than I was about baptizing Dahmer. Finally, I fell into a fitful sleep.

The next morning I was anxious to take action. Since the prison chaplain would probably not be available until after 9 a.m., I tried to busy myself with other things. Regardless, the questions and thoughts that plagued me during the night kept coming back.

Why did Jeffrey Dahmer want to be baptized? What did he know or understand about baptism? My religious body, the Church of Christ, baptizes by immersion. What problems would this pose in a prison?

The time came to call the prison chaplain, and I nervously dialed the number Rob had given me. When a guard answered, I asked for the chaplain's line. I had rehearsed my introduction before making the call, and I hoped my nervousness wouldn't keep me from being coherent.

"Hello, my name is Roy Ratcliff," I said. "I am a minister in Madison, and I received a call yesterday about one of your inmates who wants to be baptized. I'm calling to confirm that, because the inmate's name is famous."

The chaplain cut me off. "Let's cut the red tape. You're talking about Jeffrey Dahmer, aren't you?"

I was startled and swallowed before I could reply. "Yes, I am calling about Jeffrey Dahmer. I heard he wanted to be baptized, and I'm following through on his request."

The chaplain paused and said, "Yes, it's true. In fact, I have a letter on my desk that Mr. Dahmer has written me. He expressed concern about whether our prison will allow his baptism or not."

Prisons are not built with baptism by immersion in mind. I knew that many prisoners find God in prison, and that their odyssey often involves finding a way to be baptized. I wondered what the prison could provide.

But the chaplain seemed happy I'd called and glad that I was willing to deal with the request. "Perhaps," he said, "before any plans are made, you should meet with Mr. Dahmer to determine the genuineness of his desire for baptism. Then we can meet to discuss how accommodation could be made."

I was relieved. He seemed helpful.

"I do have one problem," I said. "There is a congregation closer to the prison than mine, and I feel bound to offer that minister the opportunity to baptize Mr. Dahmer."

"So, what are you suggesting?"

"I don't know just yet. Once I talk to him, either he or I, or possibly both of us, will come."

"Well, tell us who's coming," he said. "I'll need names, addresses and your official positions."

I hung up the phone and prayed. "Thank you, Father, for giving me this task, and for the part I am playing in it. If it be your will that I have no other part to play than what I have just done, may you be glorified in that. If, however, you have more for me to do, give me the wisdom to handle it."

Next, I called the minister in Baraboo, Wisconsin, a church closer to the prison. Strangely enough, his name was Jeff. He was young and was in his first ministry job. I told him the story as it had developed, and then put the question to him. "Jeff, you need to make a decision. Do you want to take care of this yourself, do you want me to take care of it, or do you want us to go together?"

I remember his answer clearly. After a short pause, he said, "I would gladly go with you." I could sense nervousness in his voice, and I could imagine his eyes growing large with the same amazement I'd seen in my church members the night before.

"We need to discuss this," I said. "A unity meeting planning session is coming up. Would you be interested in going? You could pick me up, and we could talk on the ride over."

"That would be great!" he replied. So we set the time—four days later. I couldn't call the chaplain back until I had worked out the details of our visit. I remember thinking that some things don't happen quickly.

On Monday, Jeff, the young minister, picked me up. I was anxious to discuss Jeffrey Dahmer, but first I had something I needed to ask. "I work with a Christian summer camp," I said. "I'm looking for good, quality people to serve as counselors and teachers. Would you help us this year?"

His response startled me. "I can't make that promise. We're planning to move out of state."

"What? You're planning to leave Baraboo? When?"

"We're in the process of making the final arrangements now," he said. He paused, then said, "We're having a bad time adjusting to life here in Wisconsin. We've decided to move back to New England. I can go with you to see Jeffrey Dahmer, but I'll be leaving shortly after that."

We planned the visit for the following day, but when I called the prison chaplain, I quickly learned my first lesson about prison work.

"You can't come tomorrow," he said. "The prison needs time to process the information on visitors and get permission. It will be at least another week before you can visit. Nothing happens quickly in prison. You'll just have to be patient."

We discussed possible dates and settled on April 20, 1994, for the first visit with Dahmer. But when I called Jeff, the Baraboo minister, he said, "I can't make it. I have to take my wife to the Milwaukee airport that day, and I'll be leaving the day after."

So, it was settled. Any other minister was out of the picture. I would be baptizing Jeffrey Dahmer.

In the days before my first visit, I learned more about Dahmer's desire to become a Christian. A woman in Virginia, Mary Mott, a member of my religious body, the Church of Christ, taught Jeffrey through a Bible correspondence course. I received from her a copy of the first letter she sent him, and a copy of the form he filled out requesting baptism. For several months, I thought Mary Mott had made the initial contact with Jeffrey. When the media first interviewed me about the baptism, I credited her with making the first contact.

Later, though, I learned that the prison minister in Oklahoma, Curtis Booth, who had contacted Rob McRay, was actually the first person from the Church of Christ to contact Jeffrey Dahmer. Booth sent him a Bible correspondence course and a Bible a week earlier than Mary Mott did.

When the date for my visit was set, I called Booth to assure him that Jeffrey Dahmer would be baptized. He was nervous about the whole subject and phoned me several times to urge me on. He even had others call to do likewise.

I had assured Curtis I would perform the baptism, and it wasn't until I met him sometime later that I learned why he was so nervous. He thought I wouldn't want to baptize Jeffrey because of the nature of his crimes. He had put himself in my shoes, and was acting according to the way he thought he would feel. His perception of my feelings was completely wrong.

An Oklahoma television personality had already spread the word that I was afraid to baptize Jeffrey. But I had no reluctance about performing the baptism. I was anxious about the task—partly because of the difficulties in my way and partly because I knew the expectations of others. But I wanted to get this done. I was resolved to do it.

CHAPTER 2
THE MEETING

"Your Honor, ... I know my time in prison will be terrible, but I
deserve whatever I get because of what I have done. Thank you, Your
Honor. I am prepared for your sentence, which I know will
be the maximum. I ask for no consideration."

JEFFREY DAHMER'S STATEMENT TO THE COURT, 1992

I FIRST met Jeffrey Dahmer on April 20, 1994. That day stands out vividly in my mind.

I was nervous because I am shy, and meeting new people always makes me nervous. I had never been to a prison before, and I had no idea what to expect. As I drove to the prison, my hands shook. The chaplain had given me good directions for the prison—Columbia Correction Institution in Portage, Wisconsin (about 40 miles north of Madison). I parked my car, adjusted my tie, grabbed my Bible and headed for the door.

As I walked to the main entrance, I heard a strange buzzing. What was that? Someone had seen me and was buzzing me in. Inside, I found myself in a small foyer with another locked door before me. The guard did not open the second door until the first closed behind me and locked. I reminded myself that Portage is a maximum-security prison. I entered the second door and came into a spacious waiting room with lockers on one wall, a bathroom on another, seats for visitors, a reception window and a walk-through metal detector. In the distance, I could see bars, appropriate for this prison.

At the window, I told the guard, "Hello, I'm here to visit Jeffrey Dahmer."

He pushed a paper through a slot in the window and told me to sign in—indicating the person I came to visit, who I was, the group I represented and the time of arrival. He asked for some identification, and I gave him my driver's license. He held it up to a list he had, comparing it. Apparently, I passed the test. He gave me a key with a number on it, pointed to the lockers and told me to remove everything metal from my person. Eventually, this scenario would be routine, but this first experience intimidated me.

I deposited my wallet, keys, and watch into the locker and approached the metal detector with my Bible and locker key in hand. The guard saw pens in my shirt pocket and sent me back to the locker. It didn't know pens would be a problem. Finally, I was ready for my first pass through the device.

I laid my Bible and my locker key in a small basket, and walked through. An alarm sounded! I tried again. I took my glasses off because the frames were metal. The alarm sounded again! I patted myself to see if I could find what I had missed. The guard suggested I take off my shoes. My shoes? Apparently, they had metal arch supports. Finally, in my stocking feet I passed through the metal detector successfully. What joy! I was not a threat to the prison system.

As if to congratulate me, the guard asked for my right hand. I held it out to shake his, but he turned it over and pressed a stamp onto the back. I could see no imprint. Later, I learned this stamp would show up under black light and prove that I was not an inmate trying to sneak out of prison. I was quite impressed with the barriers required just to get into the visiting area.

So now what do I do? The guard told me to wait, and after a short delay, the chaplain arrived. "Hello, my name is Gary Burkum. I'm the chaplain you talked to on the phone. I will escort you to the visiting area. Stay with me."

Obediently, I followed Chaplain Burkum. He led me through two more electronically locked doors with bars. I heard the doors shut and lock behind me. Once in the visiting area, a large room with chairs and tables, he directed me to a side room with a table and four chairs. I walked in and sat down.

"Jeffrey will be with you shortly," he said, and disappeared.

So far, this was a different scenario than I'd imagined. I didn't know what to expect, but I had seen movie and television scenes of people visiting prisoners. In those, a window separated the visitor from the prisoner, and the two talked by telephone, or perhaps through a small slot. Nothing of the sort was here. I found myself in a small room about 9 or 10 feet square with a small table and chairs.

Were they going to let me meet with Jeffrey Dahmer, the infamous murderer, face to face? Perhaps they would station a guard in the room who would be there the whole time. The minutes ticked by. I felt like I was in a doctor's examining room. I had experienced this before. Often, I arrive on time for an appointment with the doctor, but still have to wait in the waiting room. Finally, the nurse calls my name and escorts me to a small examination room. There I sit and wait and sit and wait, and begin to notice sweat trickling down various parts of my body.

It was happening again, only this time I'm in a prison, not at the doctor's office. It seemed like a long wait. I was anxious and nervous about meeting someone I had never met—someone with such a heinous criminal history. I was too nervous, even, to read the Bible. After about 7 or 8 minutes, there he was, standing in the doorway—Jeffrey Dahmer.

He was alone, with no escort, no guard, no chaplain. He looked just like he did on television, barely 6 feet tall, with blond hair and pale blue eyes. His dark green prison uniform made me think of the work clothes my grandfather bought regularly at Sears.

"Hello, my name is Jeffrey Dahmer," he said. He took a step toward me and put out his hand. I reached for it. "Hello, I'm Roy Ratcliff."

He closed the door, stepped around the table and sat down opposite me. We were all alone. Periodically, a guard would walk by and look through a window, but other than that, it was just the two of us.

Dahmer was not as big as I expected. I'm approximately 6'1", and he was shorter than I am. He was not as large as I had expected, although later he would say he had gained weight because of sedentary prison life. I looked into his eyes, and he looked back unafraid.

"I want to thank you for coming," he began. "I was afraid you might not come." As he spoke, I glanced down at his hands. They were small. Are these the hands of a murderer? They didn't look large enough to have done the damage everyone had read and heard about.

I didn't waste any time. "I understand that you want to be baptized."

"Yes, I believe it is something I need to do, but I am not certain they will allow it in this prison." I was startled—Dahmer was more concerned with the physical problems of accomplishing the baptism than he was about whether or not he should be baptized!

"Before we get into how we will do it," I said, "I need to ask you an important question. Why do you want to be baptized?"

Over the years, I've regretted baptizing people who were pushed into it by anxious parents or pressing circumstances. Baptism is important to spiritual development, and must be undertaken with the proper understanding of what it means and what is expected of the person afterward.

"Well, I used to think baptism was an optional thing, but I've done some reading and studying on the subject, and I've realized that I need to have my sins washed away, like Paul did in Damascus [see Acts 22:16, "Arise and be baptized and wash away your sins, calling upon the name of the Lord."]. In the past I picked up the idea from watching religious shows on television that baptism is not very important," Jeffrey said.

Now, he said, his view had changed. He had come to believe in the importance of baptism by studying books and pamphlets and the New Testament books of Mark, Acts and Romans. He believed he needed to be "buried with Christ," as Romans describes it. He wanted to be baptized like many were on the day of Pentecost—as reported in Acts.

Finally, he said, "I really want to be baptized."

I was surprised. Jeffrey had studied the subject beyond basic Bible correspondence courses. He was familiar with Bible passages about the subject; he understood the purpose and place of baptism. He very much wanted to address the sin in his life. He believed in Jesus Christ, and said he wanted to "put Him on in baptism"—a common phrase in my Christian fellowship.

So, he did understand the nature of baptism—and once the issue of proper understanding is settled, the issue of urgency kicks in. Such urgency is illustrated by the account of the Philippian jailer in Acts, who was baptized in the middle of the night. Once the Apostle Paul saw that the jailer had a good understanding of the need for baptism, he did not waste any time.

My decision came quickly. "Yes, I'll baptize you. It's clear that you understand what baptism is all about." When I told him this, he let out a loud sigh, an obvious feeling of relief.

"Why did you make that noise just now?" I asked. His answer has remained with me since. "I was very nervous about meeting you today," he said. "I was afraid you would come and tell me that I couldn't be baptized because my sins are too evil."

"I would never say that," I said. "Such a thought never entered my head. The whole point of baptism is dying to one's old life of sin. All sins are evil before God. I don't know of any sins too evil for Christ's blood to wash away."

In the years since our first meeting, I have been asked many questions about Jeffrey Dahmer. The most common is, "Was Jeffrey Dahmer really sincere about his baptism?" My answer always takes me back to that moment in that little room when I agreed to baptize him, and he confided his fears that I would reject his request.

I think Jeffrey was serious about his baptism. I believe people were thinking, "How could anyone who has been so sinful, who has done so many horrid things, who has walked in such wickedness ever be sincere about something like baptism?"

How unfair that question is! Will God judge the sincerity of our baptism based on our pre-Christian lives? All of us were sinners before we became Christians; all Christians have a sinful past. How would you feel about people holding you spiritually responsible for what Christ's death has removed?

Paul wrote in I Corinthians that the people in Corinth had been sexually immoral, idolaters, adulterers, male prostitutes, homosexual offenders, thieves, greedy, drunkards, slanderers and swindlers before they became

Christians. Regardless of all that, Paul said, "But you were washed, you were sanctified, you were justified in the name of the Lord Jesus Christ and by the Spirit of our God" (I Corinthians 6:11).

If previous sins call into question our baptism, then no one can be saved, including the Apostle Paul, who had persecuted and killed Christians before he accepted Jesus. When people ask this question, they are forgetting what the story of Jesus Christ is all about. To ask the question is to question the power of the blood of Jesus.

But I did have another question for Jeff. I've always found it helpful to know the religious past of any person I work with. I can anticipate the kind of questions the person will have and be prepared to address them. I asked, "What is your religious background? Do you have any religious training?" I expected him to say he had no religious experiences at all. His answer stunned me.

"My religious background is the Church of Christ," he said.

I think I made an audible gasping sound. Then I stammered, "You...you're background is the Church of Christ?" I asked, staring at him questioningly.

"Yes. My parents were both members of the Church of Christ, and we attended when I was a small child. They stopped going to church when I was 4 or 5 years old. We never went back."

"Do you know why they stopped going?" I asked.

"No. I have no idea."

"Well, tell me what experiences you've had."

"When I stayed with my grandmother in Milwaukee, I went to church with her. In fact, I really tried to get into going to church, but it was never interesting to me. Most of what I know about religion I've picked up from television."

I thanked him for his explanation. "Why don't you go back to your cell," I said, "and I'll talk to the chaplain about your baptism. When it's all settled, I'll arrange to baptize you."

Jeffrey nodded, got up and left. I followed him into the main visiting area, but didn't get far. A guard approached me, asking what I was doing. "I'm just trying to find the chaplain to talk about arrangements for a baptism," I said.

"Well, you can't walk around unescorted. Go back to the room where you were, and I'll have a chaplain come to you." I meekly obeyed and returned. Again, I had to wait and wait and wait. There goes the sweat again! Finally, a new face appeared—a different chaplain.

"Hello, my name is Gene Dawson. Chaplain Burkum is busy and can't see you. Can I help you?"

"I've talked to Jeffrey Dahmer about his request for baptism. I've agreed to baptize him, and I need to talk to someone about arranging that."

"We've discussed this," Chaplain Dawson said. "We have a question for you, too. Do you think you could have a baptistery donated to the prison? The prison system is under a strict code of equal treatment of prisoners for religious purposes. If the prison buys a baptistery for Christians, it would have to buy something of equal value for every other religious group, including a sweatbox for the Native American prisoners. We don't want to get into all that. If you could have a baptistery donated, that would work really well."

"As a matter of fact," I said, "I've been in touch with some people about prison baptisteries. I know a place that makes them, and I will see what I can find out about having one donated."

"Meanwhile, I'll be looking for a way to accommodate this request,"

Dawson said. "What size baptistery are we talking about?"

"Well, something big enough to totally immerse a grown man. We understand baptism to mean a full-body immersion in water. It would have to be big enough and deep enough to do that."

"All right," he said. "We will also need information about your church for our files. Could you send us a tract or something that tells us what your church believes?"

"Sure, I can do that," I replied. "I've got some work to do, and as soon as I find out about having a baptistery donated, I'll let you know."

I was escorted out of the visiting area and put my stamped hand under the black light. The stamped area glowed. I was allowed to pass back into the lobby.

My first visit with Jeffrey Dahmer was over, and my head was full of questions about how we would baptize him. I was certain of one thing: I would definitely baptize him!

Back at my office, the first person I wanted to contact was Curtis Booth, the prison minister in Oklahoma, to tell him I had met Jeff and had agreed to baptize him. I couldn't reach him, but a few hours later, he returned my call. "Hello, my brother! I have heard good news!" he exclaimed.

I said, "Yes, I wanted to tell you personally that I've visited Jeff and agreed to baptize him. Now, it is just a matter of working out the details."

"Let me tell you what I do," he said. "I bought a horse-watering tank, and I carry it in my pickup truck. Whenever somebody wants to be baptized, I take it to the prison, fill it up with water and perform the baptism. Why don't you do that?"

"I think I'll try getting a baptistery donated to the prison first. I've talked to people who make them, and I think that might be the best way to go for now."

"No, they'll drag their feet," Booth said. "You've got to get a watering tank and go up there and baptize him as soon as possible." Booth was pressing the urgency issue.

"The chaplains are looking for something we could use in the prison until I can find a baptistery," I explained. "I don't know what they'd think of a watering tank, and I do not really want to push the matter yet."

"You think about it, and if you decide to get one, let me know, and I'll tell you where you can find them," he said.

"I just wanted you to know that I intend to baptize Jeffrey Dahmer, and you don't need to worry about it anymore," I said, and said goodbye.

I hung up and called a friend who knew about a company in Joplin, Missouri, that makes baptisteries. I called the number he gave me and explained what I needed.

"Well, we don't just donate our baptisteries to a prison," said the man who answered. "But we may be able to find some people who will donate the cost of making one and have it sent to your prison."

By this time, I'm beginning to get used to roadblocks.

He continued, "We'll send you a picture of what we make. Essentially, it is a communion table that can be converted into a baptistery. You lift the top off, and a baptistery is inside the table."

"Okay, send me your information, and I'll pass it on."

I phoned the prison, but when I told Chaplain Burkum what I'd learned, his reply was negative. "I don't think that will work for us. We already have a communion table."

"Well, at least look at the material I'll send you about it," I said.

When the material finally came, it looked good. The top of the communion table can be removed, and inside is room for a person to be baptized. The baptistery would contain water all the time, and even had a heater to keep the water warm. I sent the brochure to the prison, and called a few days later for the chaplains' reaction.

Chaplain Burkum didn't seem excited about the whole baptism issue. "I don't think this will work for us," he said again. We already have a communion table. We don't need another one."

"What about keeping this new one in a corner or in a storage area?" I said. "Then you could bring it out when a full-body baptism was needed. What about that?"

"No, I don't think so, but I think I may have a solution. We have a whirlpool tub we use for prisoners who hurt their backs. It's about 4 feet long and 3 feet wide, and about 18 inches deep. Do you think it would work for this baptism?"

"It should work fine. When can we do it?"

"We're looking at May 10."

"I'll be there. Does it matter what time?"

"Let's shoot for 2 p.m."

"Great!"

"Oh, will we need to provide a baptismal robe?" the chaplain asked. "Or will you provide one?"

I said, "I have some here at the church building, but I don't know anything about his size, and I'm unsure of what you guys allow. Why don't you have Jeff bring a change of clothes, and he can put on dry clothes after I baptize him?"

"Don't worry, we'll figure something out," he said.

Finally, a date had been set and approved. There was nothing to do but wait for the day to come.

CHAPTER 3
DARK JOURNEY

"It's hard for me to believe that a human being could have done what I've done, but I know that I did."

JEFFREY DAHMER'S STATEMENT TO THE COURT, 1992

THE truth is our friend. That is probably the most basic lesson I have had to learn in my life. We need to know the truth. Our very lives depend upon it. But sometimes we are not comfortable learning the truth. We would rather live in ignorant bliss than in knowledge—especially when the truth is especially painful.

If you were dying of a dread disease, would you want to know? Even if you couldn't do anything about it, just knowing could help you deal with it. But, sometimes, frankly, we would rather not know.

When it comes to the subject of Jeffrey Dahmer, there is much we would rather not know. His very name makes people nervous and unsettled. Why are they so touchy? Is it because his crimes were unheard of? No. Others have murdered, dismembered, made love to the dead and even eaten human flesh. So what is so unnerving about Jeffrey Dahmer?

Could it be that too much of the truth about him came out too soon? It felt like a slap in the face. It was like being doused in profoundly cold water, so cold that you stood shivering in hot sunlight. No gradual process led to Dahmer's capture. No one was looking when they found him.

Unlike with other serial killers, there was no trail of bodies or body parts for detectives to find and speculate about. There was no profile broadcast of the "Milwaukee Monster" or some such dreadful enemy of society. Some people had gone missing, but no one had posted flyers on their behalf. Everyone expected those missing to just show up after a while.

But everything changed on July 22, 1991. That day our entire country was hit with the horrible, ghastly truth.

For most people, Jeff's story began with Tracy Edwards. As widely reported in the media and in *Step into My Parlor*, a book by Ed Bauman,[1] Edwards, a young black man, was running down West Kilbourn Avenue in Milwaukee, shortly after midnight, July 22, like a madman escaping some unknown terror.

On his arm was a pair of handcuffs clamped firmly around his wrist. Milwaukee police officers Mueller and Rauth suspected he might be fleeing an arrest and stopped. As soon as Edwards caught sight of their squad car, he ran straight to them.

For the first time in his life, Edwards, who had a troubled past, was glad to see two patrolmen. Trying to control his panic and hysteria, he begged them to take the handcuff off his wrist.

"See that building over there?" he said, pointing to the apartment in the middle of the block on the east side of 25th Street. "There's this white dude in apartment number 213, he's got a...knife stashed under his bed. He said he was goin' to cut my heart out."

The officers tried to calm him—unable to imagine the truth. They asked Edwards his story, from the beginning, and he began to recount a scenario typical of Jeffrey Dahmer's method of operation.

Earlier that evening, he said, he and a friend were hanging around the Grand Avenue mall area in downtown Milwaukee. A young white man named Jeff approached them. He invited them to his apartment for a party, and took Tracy Edwards with him to catch a cab.

Later, Edwards would learn that Dahmer pulled a switch and gave the friend a fake address.

Soon Dahmer had Edwards to himself, and made him a prisoner.

"First he starts praising me," Edwards remembers, "then he's threatening me, on and off for four hours. It was like I was confronting Satan himself. It was a four-hour period of hell."

Edwards began to sob. The apartment stank, he said, and photos of men, some naked, some dead, adorned the walls. Dahmer pressed a huge butcher knife against his chest near his heart.

In fear for his life, Edwards made his move. Dahmer happened to turn his head, and Tracy hit him with his free hand, and fled in fear.

Officers Rauth and Mueller removed the handcuff, and despite their skepticism, agreed to check out this unthinkable apartment.

The two pulled their squad car around the corner in front of 924 North 25th Street. The four-story Oxford Apartment building, long since demolished, was then a staid, orderly, yet non-descript yellow-brick structure. As they climbed the two flights of stairs, they noticed the horrific smell immediately.

Answering the knock on the door was a man with blond hair who appeared to be in his early thirties. "Are you Jeff?" they asked. "I'm Officer Mueller and this is Officer Rauth. Do you mind if we come in?"

Jeffrey Dahmer stepped aside and let them in. The officers said there had

JEFFREY DAHMER WALKS INTO THE COURTROOM AT HIS TRIAL.

been a complaint, and they wanted to look around. Jeffrey gave his permission. It was as if he had a death wish.

On entering, the officers found themselves in a basic two-room apartment with a combination living room-dining area, and a refrigerator, stove and sink taking up the entire wall nearest the door.

Rauth looked under the bed and found the knife, right where Edwards said it would be. Checking the dresser, he found one of the drawers crammed with photographs of mutilated dead bodies, photos of various body parts, and photos of graphic homosexual acts—enough to give the two policemen probable cause to search the rest of the small apartment. They were skeptical no more.

The total of what they found was beyond their worst imaginings—a human head in the refrigerator, and three more heads and a decapitated body in a small freezer. Down the hall in a closet were two human skulls. A large pot contained hands and male genitals. A 57-gallon industrial drum held three human bodies decomposing in acid. Overall, eleven victims—skulls, skeletons and body parts—were found in the apartment.

As the press reported often, Jeffrey Dahmer's victims were mostly homosexuals and minorities. He had found them at bathhouses, downtown areas and gay bars. Their sexual preference did not matter to him, or their race. His first two victims were white; the third was a Native American; the fourth and fifth were Hispanic. What attracted him most were their looks. He searched for a certain profile: men in their late teens to mid-twenties, of medium height with slender builds and smooth skin.

His method rarely varied. He discovered that weekends were best because the families would not miss the victims for a few days. He offered them money to pose nude for photographs, or invited them home for homosexual acts. Once there, he would photograph them in handcuffs and

PHOTO: ASSOCIATED PRESS

JEFFREY DAHMER WITH ATTORNEY GERALD P. BOYLE AT HIS TRIAL.

perform what he called light sex—kissing, fondling, oral sex and masturbation. He would drug his victims to unconsciousness, sexually assault them while they were asleep and finally strangle them.

As the mayhem increased, Jeffery grew weary of killing and decided to keep his victims alive. He began to experiment on some, performing makeshift lobotomies. He would drill a hole into the skull and pour acid into the brain cavity in an attempt to kill the intellect, but keep the body alive. If he were able to succeed, he wouldn't have to kill anymore. This effort never worked; they all died.

Dahmer also enjoyed cutting the bodies apart, and marveled at the colors and the glistening of the moist vital organs. What he saw fascinated him. Eventually, he tried to cook and eat some body parts. He said such cannibalism made him feel that the victims were part of him. It also gave him great sexual satisfaction.

None of us wanted to hear the horrors of this story. But Jeff needed to confess. In the end, he admitted to killing 17 young men. It is not only that he murdered so many, but also the way he did it that defies understanding. Our minds cannot comprehend such behavior. If this had occurred in some distant, primitive tribe, we wouldn't have been terribly bothered. It would still be a tragedy, but not our tragedy. This tragedy had to be dealt with. It was our tragedy. There was no mistake.

CHAPTER 4

WHY?

"Regarding your quest to better understand what led Jeff to
commit his crimes—good luck. No one knows the answer.
When I met with Jeff, it was clear to me that while he would repeat
what the psychologists had told him, he did not understand
his own actions either. On one occasion, he lamented
that the doctors had ended their study on him. He wanted
to know why he did the things he had done.
He hoped they would explain it all."

LETTER FROM ROY RATCLIFF, 2005

JEFFREY Dahmer's story, widely told in great detail, spoke of unimaginable depravity—necrophilia, murder, dismemberment and cannibalism. For Jeff, telling the story was a relief. It was cathartic. He was tired of hiding and needed to unload the secrets he had kept for so long. He desperately needed to tell all, but his need for honesty brought great pain to all who heard his story.

I believe that if we hear too much truth too soon, we have a hard time accepting it. I remember being taught how to tell someone that a loved one has died. If you come right out and say it, the relative will have a hard time facing the truth. You must build up to the awful moment. You ask the person to sit down; you say there has been an accident. It is bad. It involves a loved one who was hurt very badly. Finally, you say the person did not survive. If you pour it all out too quickly, the friend or family member will have trouble dealing with the reality.

We heard the news of Jeffrey Dahmer's crimes too quickly—escalating our shock. Yet, we still needed to hear the truth, no matter how bad it was.

I've learned that truth leans toward the light, seeking exposure. Some things can be kept a secret for a time, but truth yearns for the light and eventually the truth will be made known—even the awful truth hidden by Jeffrey Dahmer. Just as Jeffrey grew to hate the lies and the acts of hiding the truth, so do we.

I have known men who eagerly confess sexual affairs, just for relief from their lying. Lying is a burden too hard to bear. The truth is our friend, even when terrible things are revealed.

Once we understand the truth, we can make an informed response. In Jeff's case, we can try to make amends for what was done wrong—to the extent any amends are possible. But first, we must ask difficult questions. We must ask how Jeff's story came about—why Jeff's story came about.

What influenced Jeffrey Dahmer's life that accounts for his behavior? Since we cannot comprehend his actions, we question his sanity. Is there any explanation that helps us understand why he did such desperately evil things?

What do you do with an urge for something you shouldn't have or shouldn't do? It depends, of course. Eating junk food when you have a weight problem and lying to save face are not terribly harmful urges. But what if the urge is to steal or to hurt someone? What if the urge is sexual in nature and highly inappropriate—seducing another man's wife or sexually assaulting an innocent victim? What if you find yourself attracted sexually to little children? What do you do then?

Most of us would say, "You work hard to control your urges." Some desires can't be acted upon, no matter how strong the desire. Forcing yourself upon another against the person's will is a great social sin. At least in principle, society understands this.

Jeffrey Dahmer fought personal urges. When he was 14, he began to believe he was a homosexual. He was not attracted to girls, but began to have sexual fantasies. But aren't sexual fantasies typical when puberty arrives? Yes, but Jeff's imaginings were horribly awry. His thoughts of sex were intermingled with violence. As time went by, his mental agonies worsened. He didn't know who to tell—who would listen? His parents were in a long and bitter relationship that would ultimately end in divorce. He couldn't talk to them. He couldn't face disclosing such frightening images—so he simply kept them to himself.

At 15, Jeff began to collect and dissect dead animals he found by the roadside. The sight of their internal organs aroused him. His thoughts had become increasingly twisted. He began to desire to have sex with the dead. He had fantasies of killing and dismemberment. He lived in torment.

At age 17, Jeff became bolder in his efforts to satisfy his tortured mind. Once he observed a jogger in his Ohio neighborhood and thought about killing him. Several times over several days, he waited for the jogger, hiding in the bushes with a baseball bat to attack him. He planned to have sex with the man while he lay unconscious. The jogger never appeared, but Jeff experienced an anticipation he wouldn't forget.

Also at age 17, Jeff began to drink heavily—a pattern of his life for years to come. By 1978, his parents were divorcing. His father moved, and his mother took his younger brother and left Ohio for Wisconsin. Jeff was left alone in the family home at age 18, abandoned by everyone he cared for. His family members were consumed with their own problems, and no one bothered to ask about his. Soon after came his first murder.

Jeff was driving toward his house on an early evening in June 1978 when he saw a hitchhiker. Steven Mark Hicks, age 19, was on his way home from a rock concert. Jeff turned the car around, picked him up and took him home. They talked and drank some beer, and eventually, Jeff hit Steven on the head, killing him. That night, he dismembered the body and put it in garbage bags.

At 3 in the morning, he put the bags in his car to take to the dump, and strangely enough, the local police stopped him for driving left of center. When asked about the bags in the back seat, Jeff said they were garbage. The police didn't check the bags, and Jeff returned home with the body, which he hid under his house for two weeks. Later, he crushed the bones with a sledge-hammer and scattered them in the nearby woods.

No one found out what he had done. No one would know until his confession years later. His horrible journey had begun in earnest.

In 1979 after an unsuccessful semester in college, Jeff joined the army but was discharged in 1981 for alcohol abuse. Shortly thereafter, he moved in with his grandmother, Catherine Dahmer, into her neat, two-story home in West Allis, Wisconsin, outside of Milwaukee. Grandmother Dahmer was very religious and read the Bible daily, and living with her had a positive influence on Jeff for a time. Still, he wrestled with his urges and began to act upon them again.

In 1982, Jeff was convicted of disorderly conduct after exposing himself to a group of teenage boys. For several years thereafter, he tried to ignore his thoughts of sex and mutilation, but when the urges were strong, he used a male mannequin to simulate homosexual encounters. After a time his grandmother discovered the form, and made him throw it out. His necrophilial urges were becoming stronger.

In 1985, Jeffrey began frequenting gay bathhouses on Milwaukee's east side. He would take his partners to a private cubicle, drug them and have sex with them while they were unconscious.

This period was the turning point in Jeff's life according to E. Michael McCann, Milwaukee County District Attorney. Years later at Jeff's trial, he would say, "He made a conscious decision to no longer resist his evil impulses, but to yield to them. After this, no God and no law could control him. He became a law unto himself."

In 1987, nine years after his first murder, Jeff met his second victim at a gay bar. Jeff and Steven W. Tuomi, 28, went to the Ambassador Hotel and rented a room. Jeff drugged Steven to unconsciousness and intended to spend the night with him. But when he awoke in the morning, his roommate was dead. Jeff had no memory of beating the man to death, but reasoned he must have. He managed to take the body home to his grandmother's house, where he dismembered it and put it in plastic bags in the trash. His obsession with death, dismemberment and sex were uncontrolled.

Jeff killed his next two victims, James Doxator, age 14, and Richard Guerrero, age 25, at his grandmother's home. In 1988, Jeff fondled and photographed an underage male, who escaped and went to the police. Jeff was convicted of second-degree sexual assault and enticing a child for immoral purposes. While awaiting sentencing at home, he killed another victim, Anthony Sears, 24.

After serving ten months of a twelve-month sentence for molestation, Jeff moved back to his grandmother's, but in the spring of 1990 he moved into Milwaukee. He rented a place at the Oxford Apartments—924 North 25th Street.

Jeffrey took careful steps to safeguard his deeds. He installed a fake security camera. He purchased a small freezer. He felt secure in his apartment, and the pace of the killing escalated. Eleven years had passed between the first murder and the fifth murder, but the final 12 all took place in this apartment in little more than a year.

As the body count mounted, Jeff's life began to fray. When the neighbors complained about smells coming from his apartment, he made the excuse that it was the water he used in his aquarium—or meat gone bad in a broken refrigerator. A neighbor complained to the police about the odors, but officers went to the wrong apartment to check.

Jeff began to have problems disposing of the bodies. He killed too many new victims before disposing of the remains of others. During the last killings, he drank too much, took too many victims and let his job responsibilities go.

Jeff was fired from his job at the Ambrosia Chocolate Factory just two weeks before his exposure and arrest. At the same time, he was evicted from his apartment. He knew the eviction meant he couldn't keep his crimes a secret. He was going to be found out. The nightmare was coming to an end, and that end came with his arrest.

Psychiatrist Fred Berlin, who examined Jeff, diagnosed him as a necrophiliac: a person erotically aroused by thinking about or interacting with dead bodies. Dr. Berlin told Crime Stories in a television program entitled "The Life and Crimes of Jeffrey Dahmer" that the necrophilia was an irresistible urge that ultimately made Jeff kill again and again. "There was something driving him to act, that under certain circumstances, because of those circumstances, he can defer acting, but can not and was unable to stop entirely."

In the same Crime Stories episode, Dr. Park Dietz, a forensic psychiatrist who studied Jeff, agreed he was a necrophiliac, but said he didn't believe the necrophilia alone made him a serial killer. "What he did have however," Dr. Dietz said, "were three problems that account for how he would do such horrible things. The first is sexual deviations, the second is alcoholism, and the third a personality that was such that he really couldn't develop the kinds of appropriate human relationships that would have allowed him to fulfill his sexual desires without crime."

Perhaps the most revealing explanation about Jeff's behavior came from Jeff himself at the conclusion of his trial. In a video clip widely shown in the press, Jeff said, "Your Honor, it is over now. This has never been a case of trying to get free. I didn't ever want freedom. Frankly, I wanted death for myself. This was a case to tell the world that I did what I did not for reasons of hate. I hated no one. I knew I was sick or evil or both.

"Now I believe I was sick. ... I know how much harm I have caused. I tried to do the best I could after the arrest to make amends, but no matter what I did, I could not undo the terrible harm I have caused. My attempt to help identify the remains was the best that I could do, and that was hardly anything. I feel so bad for what I did to those poor families, and I understand their rightful hate.... I know society will never be able to forgive me. I know the families of the victims will never be able to forgive me for what I have done.... I am so very sorry."

Jeffrey Dahmer got his request. On February 17, 1992, he was sentenced to 15 consecutive life sentences.

What made him do it? Was it evil? Was it evil urges? Certainly, Jeffrey

Dahmer's efforts to control himself failed hideously. He needed something beyond himself—something more powerful than himself.

No one fully understands what drove Jeffrey Dahmer to commit his heinous crimes. Those on the psychiatric teams for both the prosecution and the defense admitted they did not have all the answers. Jeffrey himself wondered why he did the things he did. In truth, no one will ever be able to answer "Why?"

Imagine Jeff at the end of his trial. He had committed some of the most horrible acts recorded in civilized society. He was universally hated and despised. He wanted to die, but the state has refused to put him to death. Where could he go? Where could he turn?

Ultimately, he turned to God.

CHAPTER 5
FINDING FAITH

"If a person doesn't think that there is a God to be accountable to,

then what's the point of trying to modify your behavior to keep it within

acceptable ranges? That's how I thought anyway. I always believed the

theory of evolution as truth, that we all just came from the slime.

When we died, you know, that was it, there is nothing, and

I've since come to believe that the Lord Jesus Christ is truly God, and

I believe that I, as well as everyone else, will be accountable to Him."

JEFFREY DAHMER

INTERVIEW BY STONE PHILLIPS ON DATELINE NBC,

WHICH AIRED NOVEMBER 29, 1994, THE DAY AFTER HIS DEATH.

SKEPTICISM is often the first reaction when someone who has been profoundly evil turns to God. I've worked with other prisoners since meeting Jeff, and in almost every case, I've heard prison guards speak reproachfully of the faith of prisoners—people they see as habitual liars and cheats. They look cynically at those who find God. Yet many prisoners do come to some kind of faith. But—is that really so surprising?

In the twelve-step programs made famous by Alcoholics Anonymous, a key principle is that a person must hit rock bottom before being motivated enough to make genuine life changes. The Bible tells of the Prodigal Son, who left his home and family to live a dissolute life. After much wickedness, he ends up in a pigpen feeding the pigs, so hungry, "he longed to fill his stomach with the pods that the pigs were eating, but no one gave him anything" (Luke 15:16).

Only when the Prodigal falls so low that he has no way out does he decide to go back, to go home. Such is the rock-bottom reality that convinces a person to change.

Prison is designed to humiliate and dehumanize. Its purpose is to send a message, mete out punishment, and say, "What you did was wrong." Any hope for rehabilitation depends on the prisoner's admission that what he did was wrong. Change is required. A new way is needed.

A prisoner can grow more resentful for the treatment received in prison. Many certainly do that. Or a prisoner can develop new criminal skills and figure out how not to get caught the next time. Some also do that. Or, a prisoner can reflect on the crimes and the lifestyle that led to such a place and make a new decision: "I'll never do that again, so help me God!"

Imagine the thoughts of serial killer and mutilator Jeffrey Dahmer when he ended up in prison. He felt great remorse, which he confessed on several occasions. He had ruined his life beyond repair. If Wisconsin had the death penalty, he would have earned it. Who could he turn to except God? Certainly, no human would hear the cries of his heart and believe the depth of his sorrow. Only God could.

Jeff remembered going to church with his parents as a small child. Gradually, only his father took him, and finally, his father stopped, too. Jeff couldn't see the stress the illnesses afflicting his mother put on the marriage, nor did he hear the fights that erupted when Lionel, his father, took Jeff to church. So for years afterward, there was no church in his life.

In his adult years, when Jeff lived with his grandmother, and especially as he struggled with his internal urges to kill, he took an interest in his grandmother's church and her Christian lifestyle. But he never invested enough in her faith to ease his tortured mind or get whatever help he could for his inner Armageddon.

Eventually, he tried to justify his anomalous personality by the theory of evolution—which he viewed as antithetical to faith. He told Stone Phillips in an *NBC Dateline* interview that he had felt he didn't have to be accountable to anyone. Since man came from slime, he was accountable to no one.

Jeff's father, Lionel, often discussed evolutionary theory with him, especially after Lionel's own religious renewal in the late 1980s. Jeff's younger brother, David, had found faith while at the University of Ohio. David urged his father to return to his spiritual roots.

But after Jeffrey's arrest, a veil was lifted. He began to see order and design in the universe. He began to see the case for God and to see Jesus as the only answer for the havoc he had wreaked in his life. He began to have hope for his ultimate fate.

Is it possible that God could really love him—Jeffrey Dahmer?

Could the salvation that Jesus offers be available to him, too, despite his heinous acts? Did Jesus die for Jeffrey Dahmer, too? He began to see that the issue was not what he thought about humanity or evolution, but what he thought about God. He began to study the Bible.

While in prison, Jeff received reams of unsolicited religious materials from well-meaning people. But when Curtis Booth and Mary Mott sent him a Bible and Bible correspondence courses, he took notice. Both were members of the Church of Christ—his father's church—and the courses were produced by World Bible School, a Church of Christ ministry. He usually discarded the materials he received, but he didn't discard these.

The courses' strong evangelical message resonated with his need, and he studied and became convinced of the necessity of baptism in the salvation process. The Churches of Christ emphasize baptism as an act of faith.

Finally, after years of dissolute living, Jeffrey Dahmer, like the Prodigal

Son, decided to return to his father. He made the decision to accept Jesus Christ and signed this statement at the end of the study course:

> You have now studied enough of God's Word that you can make a decision to follow Him. You will want to continue to read and study the Bible. But now you need to make your commitment. You need to become a Christian. To do this you must obey God in the way He directs. You have now studied Faith, Repentance and Baptism. Now you need to take the step of having someone immerse (baptize) you into Jesus Christ. If this is your wish, please sign your name in this blank and your teacher will arrange to have someone in your area contact you.

Following the phrase, "I want to be immersed (baptized)—I want to become a Christian," Jeff had signed "Jeff L. Dahmer."

Instructions following said the teacher would "begin making arrangements for your baptism as soon as you make this request...."

Along with this signed request, Jeff sent messages to both Curtis Booth and Mary Mott:

Dear Mr. Booth,

> Hello, how are you today; fine I hope! Thank you very much for sending me the WBS introductory lesson and Bible; that was very kind of you! I mailed the completed lesson to Mrs. Stafford, so she should have it by now. Also, about a week after I received your package, a Mrs. Mott from Arlington, VA, sent me the WBS correspondence course, and the advanced course booklets. I filled out both of them, and mailed them off to her to be graded. So, I've now taken the complete course, but I still have one problem. This prison does not have a baptismal tank, and Mr.

Burkum, the prison chaplain, is not sure if he can find someone to bring a tank in and baptize me. This has me very concerned! Would you be willing to help find someone to baptize me? I've taken all of the other steps; now I need and want to be baptized.

Well, I hope that this letter finds you well and in good health. God bless you!

Sincerely,

Jeff Dahmer

Dear Mrs. Mott,

Hello, thank you so much for sending me the WBS correspondence course! Also, thank you for the Bible! I want to accept the Lord's salvation, but I don't know if the prison will allow me to be baptized. Mr. Burkum, our chaplain, is not sure if he can find someone to bring a baptismal tank into the prison. Would you please try to find someone that would be able to baptize me in prison? I'm very concerned about this.

I hope that this letter finds you well and in good health. God bless you!   Sincerely,

Jeff Dahmer

The letters brought joy to Curtis Booth and Mary Mott, but neither knew much about Wisconsin geography. Both began a frantic search to find someone, anyone, who would be willing to baptize Jeffrey Dahmer.

CHAPTER 6
THE BAPTISM

"Here is a trustworthy saying that deserves full acceptance: Christ Jesus came into the world to save sinners—of whom I am the worst. But for that very reason I was shown mercy so that in me, the worst of sinners, Christ Jesus might display his unlimited patience as an example for those who would believe in Him and receive eternal life."

I TIMOTHY 1:15-16 NIV,

READ BY JEFFREY DAHMER IN HIS STATEMENT TO THE COURT, 1992

THE tenth of May finally arrived.

My appointment at the prison was set for 1 p.m., an hour before the baptism. I would spend the extra time privately with Jeff. During this time, I would take Jeff's confession of faith in Jesus Christ. I knew that Jeff believed on Jesus as the Christ, the Son of God, but tradition dictated that I formally ask him. After our brief meeting, we would be escorted to the baptism area.

As I drove to the prison that day, I wondered about Jeff's emotional state. Was he nervous about being baptized? Did he fully comprehend what we were about to do? We had discussed the need for baptism, but in all the excitement, the subject of his past sins had not even come up. Did he understand that baptism serves to bring assurance that Christ's blood "washes away sins"? Would he appreciate this biblical truth? I have baptized many, many people who have not appreciated the fact that their sins were washed away. Would Jeff struggle with a sense of guilt after his baptism?

Two events dominated the news that day. The first was a near-total solar eclipse. The second was the execution of another well-known serial killer, John Wayne Gacy. As has become a common ritual, many men and women on the street were asked for an opinion about the two events occurring on the same day. I couldn't listen to a radio station or watch a television program without seeing an anonymous person crying about the appropriateness or inappropriateness of having an execution on a day we were experiencing a solar eclipse.

The subject of capital punishment is an emotional one—and one that resurfaces whenever a prisoner is put to death. The fact that an execution was occurring during a solar eclipse brought a strange poetry to what I heard that day. For those against public executions, the solar eclipse was a message from God. He would not allow the sun to shine on such a deplorable act. For those in favor of Gacy's death, the eclipse was a strangely appropriate sign of the evil he had done—and again was a message from God. In this view, the darkness reflected God's condemnation of Gacy and of what lay in store for him in the next life. Strange commentary!

As I listened, I wondered what these people would say if they knew what I was about to do on this day.

Rather than end a life, I was hoping to assist in a new birth. I would help a man prepare to meet his God by dying to his old sinful self. Would some see this as reason for the sun not to shine? Would they be embarrassed and ashamed that such a heinous criminal would embrace a faith like their own?

The full effect of the eclipse was eerie. The noon sky was dark and dusky when I arrived at the prison. The gloomy scene could easily be interpreted as an omen of bad to come. But I was on my way to do something good, very good. Who could dwell on bad things to come?

Later, I learned how dark and grim the hearts of some people were when they learned of Jeff's baptism, and I would remember the darkness of that day. The day a person is baptized is a day of great joy and celebration. But many who claim to wear the name of Christ did not rejoice with gladness of heart when they heard of Jeff's conversion.

I never heard these, but others reported to me comments they'd heard, like: "If Jeffrey Dahmer is going to heaven, then I don't want to be there." What a dark and horrible thought. Thinking of it takes me back to that afternoon and the cast of the sky before I went inside the prison.

Once again, I went through a complicated process to gain entrance. The procedure would become more tolerable as weeks and months went by, but for now it was a burden. Today, Chaplain Burkum was waiting for me at the door, enabling me to go through a little faster. He escorted me to a special conference room, not the small room on the right of my first visit, but a larger room on my left with a bigger table and several chairs. I waited nervously for Jeff to arrive. When Jeff finally arrived in his prison uniform, he was excited.

"I guess we're going to have a baptism," I said.

"Really? I haven't heard a thing until the chaplain told me you were here. I was wondering if the baptism was not going to be allowed. But, since you're here, I guess it's okay." I never have understood why the prison chaplains kept Jeff in the dark about his own baptism date.

"Jeff, sit down for a few minutes," I said. "This is probably obvious, but I need to be sure you understand that baptism has something to do with your sins. Do you understand what baptism does to your sins?"

"Oh yes, I know it washes away my sins. If anyone needed to have his sins washed away, it is me! In fact, I'm looking forward to it and counting on it."

"Good," I continued. "I need to ask you another thing, too. Do you believe that Jesus is the Christ, the Son of God?"

He smiled as he gave his answer. "Yes, I believe that Jesus is the Christ, the Son of God. In fact, I've said so lots of times in the various interviews I've given to the media, but each time, when the report airs, that part is left out."

"I guess this is the price of my infamy." He rolled his eyes heavenward. He would speak of his "infamy" on several occasions, always using that same facial expression.

"Well, I do have a question for you," he countered. "Something is bothering me because of what other prisoners have said, and I wanted to ask you about it. What are you planning to say when you baptize me?"

"Do you mean the words?" I asked.

"Yes. I've been told it really matters," he replied.

"Well, I have always used the words of Jesus at the end of the book of Matthew (28:19). I intend to say that I am baptizing you 'in the name of the Father and of the Son and of the Holy Spirit.' Was that what you were expecting?"

"Well, I've heard from other inmates that baptisms that use those words aren't valid. The only words should be, 'I baptize you in the name of Jesus.' I don't know anything about this, but I want everything to be right."

"Let me assure you. I've performed many, many baptisms. I don't see any difference in the words. If you want me to use those words, I'll be glad to do that."

"No, no, I don't really care which words you use. My only concern is that everything be done right."

"Let me tell you—your baptism will be done right. Since you don't mind which words I use, I'll use what I usually say. But you don't need to worry about your baptism not being valid. God understands what we are doing, and, personally, I feel more comfortable using those very words of Jesus."

Chaplain Burkum returned before we were to be escorted to the whirlpool. "If redemption is what you want," he said, "you might consider what the Moslems do here in prison. They believe that by simply rubbing their hands against a rough surface, like the wall of the prison, that they can gain redemption. Have you ever considered doing this instead?"

I was shocked to hear this. I looked at Jeff, and he looked at me with the same look of unbelief. How could a chaplain who claims to be a Christian suggest that we follow a Moslem custom for gaining redemption? Was he trying to stop this baptism before it could occur? I've never understood why he said this.

I spoke first. "No, I think we'll go on with Christian baptism rather than follow the Moslem practice." As I spoke, Jeff nodded his head in agreement. By his body language, I could tell he was grateful that I answered.

The chaplain left to call the guards to escort us to the medical facility and whirlpool tub. On our way, we passed other inmates walking the other way. They carried mops and brooms and were followed by a guard.

I didn't know if inmates were allowed to speak to each other—I'd gathered that the rule was silence. But this was an exceptional day, so perhaps leniency was allowed. One of the prisoners called out, "Hey, J.D., how's it going?"

Jeff was in bright spirits. He answered, "Great! I'm going to be baptized today!" The other inmates faces lit up, and one of them began humming a gospel tune, setting the stage for a sense of joy that was to pervade the whole experience.

Neither the guards nor the chaplain rebuked the inmates or Jeff for his reply. They seemed to recognize that something special was going to happen. The guards continued walking—one leading the way, Jeff following, the chaplain and I behind Jeff, and one guard behind us all. No one spoke again.

When we reached the medical area, I looked in and saw the whirlpool. "This should do just fine," I said. The chaplain held up a white polyester robe that someone had made—obviously for a baptism. I remembered the chaplain's concerns about a baptismal garment, and I've always wondered if it had been used before, or was made for Jeff.

A guard remained in a little room where Jeff would change clothes. The chaplain, the other guard and I stepped out into the hallway.

As we waited, the joy of this special occasion grew. Both the chaplain and the guard in the hallway began to tell stories of baptisms. I'd seen this before—the baptismal experience is so real and fundamental that it brings to mind similar experiences. It is a tender moment when the soul seems to touch the divine.

I was intrigued to hear their stories and began to share mine. Each memory was about beautiful and wonderful experiences—it was amazing.

The door to the little room opened. Jeff was ready to be baptized. I was surprised to see that he had already climbed into the tub, and he turned around a couple of times to figure out how it all would work. The tub was fairly small, and he would have to assume a fetal position in order to fit in all the way.

When he was ready, I placed my hands on his head and one shoulder. I said, "Jeff, upon your confession of faith in Jesus as the Christ, the Son of God, I now baptize you in the name of the Father and of the Son and of the Holy Spirit for the forgiveness of your sins."

I pushed him under the water until he was completely immersed. When his head broke the surface, I said something I always say when I baptize someone. "Welcome to the Family of God!"

He looked at me with a smile of gladness and surprise, and said simply, "Thank you." He climbed out of the tub and took a towel to dry off. The chaplain, a guard and I stepped out into the hall as he changed into dry clothes.

Again, we told of baptismal experiences, and this time the chaplain spoke movingly of his daughter's baptism. The mood was reverential and sacred, and I felt a sense of spiritual bonding with these two men as we waited. The walk back to the chaplain's office seemed to go quickly. I was happy to see the bounce in Jeff's step; he was obviously filled with joy.

Before Jeff was returned to his unit, I made a special appeal to the chaplain. "I would like to visit with Jeff on a regular basis. I want to help him develop his faith. I don't want to just slip out of his life. I'd like to see him every week to study the Bible."

As I spoke, the chaplain nodded his head in agreement, but Jeff had a shocked look on his face. "I just thought you would leave, and I'd never see you again," he said.

"No, I won't leave you. If I can, I would like to visit every week to study with you."

"That would be wonderful!" Jeff said.

Chaplain Burkum was willing to set up a visitation plan. "I'll set up what we call a permanent pastoral visitation. What day would you like to come each week?"

"Wednesdays would work fine with me," I replied.

"Good. Wednesdays will be your day, and I can set it up for tomorrow, if you like."

"No, not tomorrow," I said, "but let's set it up for next week."

I had another request of the chaplain. "The woman who sent Jeff the correspondence course has asked if she can come to visit Jeff. Can this be arranged, too?"

Chaplain Burkum asked if the woman, Mary Mott, was on Jeff's visitor's list. She wasn't. Jeff knew her only through the correspondence course.

"Well, is she an officiate of the church?" the chaplain asked. No, she was a church member who sent out Bible correspondence courses throughout the world. The chaplain would consider her a layman.

"Then such a visit is out of the question," he said. "We don't allow just anyone to come visit our prisoners, especially famous ones like Jeffrey Dahmer. Why, even you could not come to see him if he had not requested it. You couldn't come here and say, 'I would like to visit Jeffrey Dahmer, please.' Only when a prisoner makes a request to see someone like you do we allow it. Someone like her, who is not on his visitor's list, and who is not an officiate of the church, can't come."

"Well, I didn't know all that. She has already arranged airline tickets to come visit Jeff, and I'll have to tell her she can't come. I'm sure she'll be disappointed."

"If Jeff wants to add her to his visitor's list, he could do that, but it will take about six months to process."

Jeff wasn't interested in adding Mary Mott to the list. He thought it too complicated, and he would have to take someone off his visitor's list to make room for her. I asked Jeff to write her to explain.

My time to leave had come. I had accomplished what I came for. Jeffrey Dahmer had been baptized and a weekly appointment set so that we could study the Bible together. I hoped to study the Gospel of John and the life of Jesus with him.

The effects of the eclipse were finished when I left the prison and got into my car. Despite the solar eclipse and the Gacy execution, it had turned out to be a wonderful day. I felt happy and fulfilled. It was a beautiful drive home.

When I got home, I had a phone call to make. One of the women in my congregation had heard I was going to baptize Jeffrey Dahmer, and asked that I call her when I returned from the prison. She worked for a news agency and thought the baptism would be newsworthy. I didn't think it was anyone's business, but at her urging, I had agreed. I told her, "Barbara, I baptized Jeffrey Dahmer today. I know you wanted to know when it happened." She was glad to hear the news and congratulated me for the baptism. She thanked me for the phone call. I was quite naïve about what would follow.

CHAPTER 7
THE MEDIA

"Is there no joy in knowing that a sinner has turned

to God? A gross misunderstanding of what was

accomplished by Jeff's baptism was apparent.

No one said Jeff was no longer guilty of his crimes.

He would not be released from prison, nor should he be,

dependent on his baptism. Baptism does not take away

crimes. It addresses sins. The issue in baptism doesn't concern

justice in the society. It concerns the forgiveness of God."

ROY RATCLIFF

THE 11th of May started out as any other day in spring. The weather was getting warmer as summer approached. The grass was getting greener with every passing day. The songbirds were singing. Windows and screen doors were open—airing out winter and bringing a refreshing scent.

It started out as such a beautiful day. It was the day after Jeff's baptism, and my spirits were high. But the beauty of the day was deceiving. This day would bring a dramatic turnaround from yesterday's events. I was to experience my own eclipse with both darkness and brilliant light.

I arrived at my office a little after 9 a.m. and started sorting through the mail. It was a Wednesday, so I needed to get ready for Bible classes that night. Barbara, the church member who works for the news agency, called me at 9:30 to read what she had written about Jeff's baptism.

At that time, I didn't really understand the nature of Barbara's job. To me, she was simply a member of my congregation who found the story appealing and wanted to write about it. She didn't mention my name in her release and covered only the basic facts. Her report was short and simple: "Jeffrey Dahmer was baptized in a whirlpool at Columbia Correctional

Institution, Portage, Wisconsin, on May 10, 1994, at 2 p.m. A minister from Madison performed the baptism."

She asked me what I thought of it. "It sounds fine to me. You got all the facts correct," I said.

She said, "Roy, I have a very important question to put to you right now. You may want to give some thought to your answer."

"Oh? What is that?" Little did I know my answer would affect my life drastically in coming days.

She said, "You don't seem to understand that this is big news."

"You're right. I don't see this as anything news people would find interesting."

"Well, trust me; they're going to jump right on this story. As soon as I release it, my office will be flooded with requests for your identity. I'm asking for your permission to release your name."

"Why would you need my name?" I asked very naïvely.

"Well," she began to explain patiently, "without your name, the story lacks credibility. It will be dismissed as a ridiculous rumor and become the fodder for jokes. On the other hand, releasing your name would give the story credibility, but it will put you under the scrutiny of the press. You will likely be hounded for several days by reporters from the newspapers and television and radio."

I must admit; that did not sound appealing.

Barbara continued to press her point. I'd conducted a Bible study in her home for several years, and she understood my great concern for the world to hear the gospel. She said, "You've always said that one of the greatest needs of our society is to hear the simple story of Jesus Christ, but people are generally not interested in hearing it. Well, nothing will grab the attention of people who need Jesus as much as Jeffrey Dahmer's baptism. You can share the simple story of salvation with literally thousands of people. But the price you will have to pay will be the sacrifice of your privacy."

"Well," I replied, "you are making a strong case."

"And more than that," she said. "Jeff's story is a profound example of God's grace toward a sinner. Jeff's story illustrates grace. If the world needs to hear anything, it needs to hear about God's grace."

I had to smile as I listened to her. Here she was preaching to me, the preacher. Just barely two years before this, I had shared the concept of God's grace with Barbara and rejoiced over her baptism. Here she was giving it all back to me. She had made her point. I decided to release my name—for Jeff, but also for Barbara. She needed to see that my actions and my convictions were consistent.

"All right, you've made your case," I said. "You can release my name if anyone asks for it. I still don't see why this would be much of a story. I don't think anybody in the world would care whether Jeffrey Dahmer was baptized or not. But, I'll let you go with the item you've written."

We said our good-byes and hung up.

I sat there for a few seconds reflecting on what we'd said. I had no interest in making a name for myself. Barbara was blowing this whole thing out of proportion. No one would care about this.

But—how wrong I was. In less than five minutes, the phone rang. It didn't stop for days.

The first call was a reporter for our local newspaper, the Wisconsin State Journal. "Is it true," he asked, "that you baptized Jeffrey Dahmer?" When I told him it was true, he wanted to send a reporter out to interview me and take my picture. A picture? I had not even thought about a picture.

"Let's schedule it for 1 this afternoon," I said, putting it off until I could run home and grab a coat and a tie. One of the nasty truths about being a minister, at least in 1994, was that people expected you to look like a minister—with a coat and a tie. When I was in my office and not planning to see anyone that day, I usually dressed casually. If I visited people in the hospital or at their homes, I'd wear "the outfit." For a picture in the newspaper, I had to look the part. I hung up, and the phone rang again. It was another reporter, this time from a magazine. Then there was a call from a radio personality, who wanted to do a phone interview. Local television stations called. I tried to deal with each one as openly and honestly as I could.

Around 11:30, I fled the office and drove home to get changed and grab lunch. I didn't want the media to hunt me down at home, and I needed to warn my family to refer callers to my office.

Of course, that warning didn't hold. Reporters came after me at all hours. One television station wanted me to appear on the 5 o'clock news. I met with reporters in my office and at the church building. I was photographed, videotaped, and recorded. They wanted to know my every detail. One television newsmagazine even photographed the car I drove to the prison! It was ridiculous, but I tried to accommodate them as well as I could.

One interview with a radio announcer stands out in my mind. He had callers ask me questions. One asked if I would allow Jeffrey Dahmer to babysit my children. I thought that was a strange question and could not understand why he would even ask it.

"It has to do with forgiveness," he explained. "If Jeffrey Dahmer has been truly forgiven, and all his past sins are forgotten, then why wouldn't you allow him to baby-sit your children?"

"There is a whole lot more involved than that, but if I understand your point correctly, you are asking if Jeffrey Dahmer has been forgiven of all his sins. To that I would say, yes, he has. Whether he would be a qualified person to baby-sit children is another question entirely," I replied.

I could see that people were confused about what forgiveness means. The most common question I heard from the reporters was whether I thought Jeffrey Dahmer should be released now that he has been baptized. Foolish question! So many people are confused about what forgiveness of sins means. They cannot distinguish crimes against the state and sins against God—which probably reflects the general vision people have about God.

Among the callers was an angry Chaplain Burkum. He seemed to think I had intentionally sought media coverage. "What have you done? Are you trying to make a name for yourself? If I had known you would exploit Jeffrey Dahmer this way, I wouldn't have allowed you to see him in the first place." He was very angry with me, and I got the impression that Jeff shared his perspective.

I could deal with the chaplain's anger, but I was deeply concerned about Jeff's feelings. From my point of view, I did not intentionally seek media coverage, it just happened. I couldn't believe that Barbara's little news release would have this response. I called her to tell her the baptism had taken place simply because she asked me to. This situation had developed a life of its own.

"I'm sorry this has happened. It was not my intention for anyone to know about it," I told the chaplain.

"Well, then how did the news media find out about it?" he demanded.

"I mentioned it at church, and one of the women in the church works at a news agency, although I didn't really know what her job was. She had asked me to call her after I baptized Jeff. When I did, she wrote a press release. I didn't expect things to develop as far as they have."

My explanation did not appease him. "You should have known better. This is your fault!" he said as he hung up. I knew I was in trouble.

I wondered if the chaplain would interfere with my pastoral visitations at the prison. I imagined Jeff had seen the newscast. All of the members at church had seen it and were talking about it that Wednesday night.

Did Jeff see me as a preacher hungry for publicity and eager to exploit his name? I knew I had to do something. I didn't think I could call Jeff on the phone (actually, I probably could have, but I didn't know much about prisons then). I would write him a letter.

My note was brief, but heartfelt. "I want you to know I never thought things would develop the way they have. I believe, regardless of what I have done, that the story would have reached the media anyway. I'm sorry for my part in all of this, but I really don't know how else I could have dealt with the situation.

"Chaplain Burkum has implied that you are as angry with me as he is over all this. If that is true, then you may not want to see me at our next appointed time. I still intend to come this next Wednesday to see you. If you don't want me to visit you any more, I want you to tell me that to my face.

"If you feel you cannot trust me, I will voluntarily stop my visits with you, but I will try to arrange for someone else, another minister, to take my place. It is very important to me that you receive visits to strengthen your new faith. Once again, I am very sorry; it was not my intention to bring you more publicity."

I sent the letter off, and nervously waited for a reply. None came, so I went ahead and drove up to the prison for our next appointed visit. Finally, I got inside and was able to see Jeffrey. I told him, "When Chaplain Burkum called me and expressed his disappointment in me, it sounded like you felt that way, too. That's why I wrote you the letter."

His reply was a comfort to me. "No. I'm proud of you for telling the world that I believe in Jesus Christ. My main complaint with the media is that in every interview I speak of my faith, but when the interviews are aired, they cut that section out. I'm glad that you were able to tell the world that I am a believer!"

To my face, no one has ever said anything negative about my baptizing Jeffrey Dahmer. I don't know if this reflects general dishonesty in people or not. I did hear about people who had talked with me about the baptism, but later had terrible things to say on the subject. One story really sticks in my mind.

He called the morning the news got out about Jeff's baptism. He was a local radio personality who had a reputation for outlandish shows and ranting and raving about the latest issue. I didn't know what to expect when I heard from him. I expected him to start raving at me! To my surprise, he was respectful during a phone interview. I was impressed and willingly retold the story of Jeff's baptism.

Later I found out that he started throwing temper tantrums right after I was on the air. He belittled Jeff's baptism and mocked his faith. He cried out again and again, saying that if Jeffrey Dahmer could be forgiven for his crimes, then it really didn't matter what anybody does because horrible crimes could always be forgiven. He was respectful to me to my face, but far different behind my back.

Such an incident was typical of my media experiences. The interviewers would be respectful, and at times, amazed at my story. Sometimes that respect carried into their stories. But often, the reporters I talked with sounded far different in the interviews than in their news reports. The words came from the same person, but the attitude had changed from civility to harsh criticism and cynicism. The reporters passed on their attitudes to the average person.

I felt a dark cloud had begun to surround me, but was keeping its distance so I was not completely aware of its presence. I learned of the dark attitudes and profound disapproval of people only by talking with friends and church members. All I saw firsthand was wonder, amazement and admiration for my baptizing Jeff.

Once, when I was visiting Jeff, a guard told me about the controversy I had caused in his church as the members were having a hard time accepting the idea of Jeffrey Dahmer as a Christian.

Sometime later, I visited a man in the hospital who recognized me from the press coverage. He was a Christian college student at the time of Jeff's baptism. The thing he remembered most was a comment by one of the instructors in a hallway. It probably captured the sentiment of many: "If Jeffrey Dahmer is going to heaven, then I don't want to be there."

How can a Christian hold that viewpoint? I don't understand it. Does it come from a misunderstanding of the forgiveness of sin? Is forgiveness limited to those who are not very bad after all?

Is there no joy in knowing that a sinner has turned to God? A gross misunderstanding of what Jeff's baptism accomplished was apparent. No one said Jeff was no longer guilty of his crimes. He would not be released from prison, nor should he be, dependent on his baptism. Baptism does not take away crimes. It addresses sins. The issue in baptism doesn't concern justice in the society. It concerns the forgiveness of God.

I suppose I can understand the anger felt by some people about Jeff's baptism. They feel justice has been cheapened or ignored. The whole point of justice is to make things right. What about justice? How does it fit into this picture?

Forgiveness is all about the mercy of God, and the nature of mercy sometimes leaves the feeling that justice has been violated. That's not true. There is a profound relationship between justice and mercy. Justice without mercy is unreasonable, and mercy without justice is meaningless. The two must exist together, and each must reflect the truth of the other.

The mercy offered in baptism exists because of Jesus' death on the cross, which fulfilled God's demand for justice. Jesus died for our sins because justice demands death as the payment for sin. Those who reject the mercy of God must deal with the untempered justice of God in his wrath against sin.

Jeff's crimes cry out for justice. People seethe with righteous indignation when they think of his horrible deeds. He needs to suffer for the crimes he committed. Hence, they believe, hell is the proper place for Jeffrey Dahmer.

No one understood this quite as well as Jeff. He understood that it was from the anger and wrath of God that he sought redemption. Baptism is about salvation and the redemption of the soul. It relates only to our relationship with God. It does not address justice issues of the state. It does address justice issues of God.

It became very clear to me as I experienced my "15 minutes of fame" that many people cannot distinguish between justice and salvation, and between what the state does and what God does. God is not the state, and the state is not God; the two govern different realms.

Some people related to me differently after the media blitz. Once, my father-in-law introduced me to a man he knew in Milwaukee, saying, "Do you know what he did?" Once my relationship with Jeff was mentioned, the man walked off and left us in silence. I felt very alone. That happened a lot.

Even church people I'd known for years would say to others, "Do you know what he did? He's the man who baptized Jeffrey Dahmer." And then the silence would follow. I never knew whether they were proud of me, or ashamed. I lived in my own eclipse for a long time, for Jeff's baptism overshadowed everything about me. But eventually, the sun returned.

For a week after Jeff's baptism, I saw my name and my face plastered all over television and in newspapers and magazines. I was glad when the blitz ended. I looked forward to my visits with Jeff and the beginning of a new ministry—in prison.

CHAPTER 8

DEEP GRACE

Wherefore the law was our schoolmaster to bring us unto Christ,
that we might be justified by faith. But after that faith is come, we are no longer
under a schoolmaster. For ye are all the children of God by
faith in Christ Jesus. For as many of you as have been baptized into
Christ have put on Christ. There is neither Jew nor Greek, there is
neither bond nor free, there is neither male nor female:
for ye are all one in Christ Jesus.

GALATIANS 3:24-28 KJV

I HAD been looking forward to May 18 with a mixture of apprehension and excitement. This would be my first meeting with Jeff after the baptism, and I was anxious to address several things.

"What will you talk about?" one of my church members asked.

"Well, I don't really know, but I would like to talk to Jeff about Jesus as I understand him, and allow the vision of Jesus to mold him into a mature Christian."

"Well, what about the Lord's Supper? How can he take that every Sunday?" the man asked, citing a key tenet of the Churches of Christ. "What about the instrumental music question? How can he worship in prison with musical instruments?" he pressed.

My response was naïve. "I don't think these issues will be a big deal since Jeff hasn't been involved with the Churches of Christ all that much," I said. "He attended as a small child, but it's unlikely he has absorbed much of the controversy on these subjects. I'm not expecting those issues to even come up."

I was wrong on both counts. These issues, so important to many in the Churches of Christ, would, indeed, concern Jeffrey Dahmer. I wanted to give him a simple faith in Jesus Christ and protect him from some of the arguments and controversies that have raged within my faith, but that was not to be.

Jeffrey came from a life of almost unimaginable depravity to accept Jesus Christ. Why, why would he be concerned with the fine points of any religion? I've learned since that time that people who have committed the worst possible acts are often the most concerned with adhering to the finest points of religious doctrine. Why? Perhaps they are seeking security from their terrible impulses in a rigid belief system. Perhaps they, more than most people, just want to be certain of their justification before God.

Convincing Jeffrey that God brings grace to the sinner, not a straitjacket of laws, was to be a challenge. And one I didn't expect.

Most likely, I was overly concerned that Jeff was disillusioned with me for my part in the media coverage. I didn't want to imagine digging through a litany of conflict-ridden doctrine with him. Above all, I didn't want to alienate him.

I did fear he would agree with what Chaplain Burkum had said about the media reports. Yet, I could not put off seeing him. If he never wanted me to visit him again, he would have to tell me to my face. If that were his decision, I planned to stress his need for someone to study with him, and make connections with someone to come in my place.

I arrived at the prison at the appointed time, went through the tedious entry procedure, was escorted to a private room and told to wait until Jeff was called. The minutes passed and my nervousness increased.

What would I do if Jeff told me he didn't want to continue the visitations? Who would I find to work with him? Could I persuade him of my good intentions? Would he understand my naiveté and inexperience with the media? Would he be open to a study of the person and character of Jesus? The more I thought, the more anxious I became. When he finally arrived, I was a bundle of nerves.

"I'm so glad you came," he began. "I really wanted to tell you that I do not feel the way Chaplain Burkum does. I'm happy you let the world know that I was baptized."

My relief was enormous. "Chaplain Burkum was really angry with me over all the coverage, and he seemed to imply that he had spoken with you and that you agreed with him," I said.

"No," Jeff said. "He never talked with me about it. I saw you on the television! I have heard my name on television a lot, and I'm used to hearing all kinds of stuff about myself. But I didn't expect anyone to care that I was baptized," he explained.

"Well, I was worried about how you felt about me and my part in all that. I didn't have a chance to talk with you on the phone to get your initial reaction. I hadn't thought it would bother you until I heard from the chaplain, but after his phone call I was concerned," I answered.

"You are the first person to ever say publicly that I believe in Jesus, and I thank you for that," he said.

"I will not leave you or desert you," I told him. "I'm committed to help you grow and learn as a Christian. As far as I'm concerned, I will keep coming to study with you until one of us dies."

Funny. I expected a confrontation, an angry argument, possibly even a dismissal. Instead, Jeff encouraged me. I cannot convey how deeply relieved I was to hear his words. Likewise, he came expecting me to say I wouldn't be coming again because of the chaplain's rebuke. Instead, he heard me say I was committed to continuing to work together.

So we were accepting of each other before we knew what our spiritual relationship meant. But I didn't get an opportunity to suggest we study the nature of Jesus in the Gospel of John. Before I could say, "What would you like to study?" or "Here is what I think we should study," Jeff started off with questions.

He was absolutely full of questions. He had stored them up, and now he had someone willing to listen to him and answer them. He didn't want to waste a moment of the opportunity. His questions would drive our discussion and study for several weeks.

"What do I do about the Lord's Supper?" he asked first.

I was stunned. "What do you mean?" I asked. As I've said, I was naïve to think he wouldn't know of the Church of Christ's practice of weekly communion.

"Well, they offer church services every Sunday here in prison," he explained. "But the services are by different denominations, and don't offer the Lord's Supper. It is only available once a month. If I need to have the Lord's Supper every Sunday, how am I going to do that?"

I started to answer, but he quickly cut me off.

"I've done some thinking. I have a supply of crackers in my cell, which I could use for the bread. I also have some dry grape drink mix I could use for the wine. Would that be okay?" he asked cautiously.

"Yes, I would think that would be fine," I replied.

"The reason I ask is I've read a lot about this. I get a lot of stuff in the mail. Most of it is not asked for, but I have read about the Lord's Supper. I've read that only freshly squeezed grape juice is allowed, but I can't get freshly squeezed grape juice in prison! I can't get even bottled grape juice, or wine or frozen grape concentrate. All I can get is this grape drink mixture that you just add water to. I can make this up in my cell. Would that be all right with God?" he quickly poured out.

It was obvious this matter really bothered him. He had spent much time wrestling with this and needed reassurance.

I said, "Look, many views exist about the Lord's Supper, and many of those views don't make sense for you here in prison. If you weren't in prison and able to go to church, you would take whatever was offered, and probably not even think about it. But given your setting, some of the practices you've heard about are simply out of the question."

"Yeah, I know. I don't know what to do," he replied.

"Well, you shouldn't worry. I believe God understands your situation and knows what you are capable of doing. As for this law about using freshly squeezed grape juice, I've been in the church for many years and preached for many years, and I have never heard of such a thing. That is utter nonsense as far as I'm concerned.

"I don't believe God will hold you responsible if you can't obtain the things you need to serve him. God is a gracious God, and a compassionate God and a God of understanding. He knows your situation and what you are dealing with. I don't think it matters to God whether the grape drink is dried and mixed with water, or is freshly squeezed, or is bottled or frozen. What matters is that you have set your heart to serve God and obey Him as much as possible."

"Well, I just want to do everything right. I've lived my life in the wrong ways long enough. I just want to do what is right as far as God is concerned," he said.

"God understands what you're facing," I said, "and he looks into your heart. He will judge fairly. You don't need to worry."

"Okay. You've convinced me. When I can't take communion in the church services, I'll take it in my cell."

His second question was even more surprising than the first one. "What translation of the Bible should I use? What translation do you use?" he asked.

Again, I entered the discussion naively, not knowing that he already had a version in mind. "I use the New International Version. I have studied the Greek and the Hebrew languages, and I've studied the different translations in terms of accuracy and readability. It is very important that a translation is accurate, but it's equally important that the message be understandable in the clearest language possible. In the end, I finally settled on the New International Version."

By the look on his face, I could tell my answer did not sit well with him. "Well, I use the King James Version," he said. "Everything I've read tells me that this is the only reliable version of the Bible and that the Greek text the King James translation is based on is superior to all other Greek texts. Why would you use any other translation?"

"Don't you find the King James translation hard to read in places?" I asked.

"Well, yes, but that's not the point. For me the issue is accuracy, and I believe the King James is the most accurate Bible translation."

I tried to proceed gently. I said, "Well, there is a lot of debate on that issue. There are problems with the King James version because so many of the English words have changed their meaning since that translation was made."

"What do you mean?" he asked.

"A number of words mean just the opposite today from what they meant in 1611. One example is the word, 'let.' Paul uses it in Romans to say that he intended to come to them, but Satan 'let' him. What he means is that Satan hindered him. This use of the word 'let' is found today only in tennis, when a ball is stopped by the net is a 'let' ball. Today, the word has the meaning of 'to allow,' not hinder. The King James has many words like that, and I find myself spending half my time needing to redefine the words in order to understand the message."

"Okay," he said. "But what about its accuracy?"

"Well, all Bible translations are based on Greek manuscripts. None go back to the original; all are copies, and most are copies of copies of copies. The oldest and most reliable complete manuscripts date only to the 400 A.D. era. Nearly all of these were either not discovered at the time of the King James translation, or were not available.

"The Greek text the King James Bible is based on comes from newer, not older manuscripts. Most people consider the Greek text used for the King James Bible to be inferior, not superior to modern-day Greek texts."

Jeff was flabbergasted. "This can't be! I have read books that have assured me that the Greek text of the King James Bible is superior to all other Greek texts."

I decided to move on. "Look, we're not going to settle this question here and now. We don't have the resources to get into this like we ought to. I propose that you use the King James Bible. You obviously have a lot of confidence in it. I will continue to use my New International Version. If there are disagreements, and I doubt there will be many, we can compare them and decide as best we can from what we have studied what is right. How does that sound?"

"I guess that will be okay," he answered cautiously.

"Jeff, translation differences are usually over minor points. The main ideas and concepts of God are revealed in both translations. We'll gain by studying together."

"Okay. I see your point. That will just have to be the way it is."

The last question Jeff raised is a highly debatable one in my Christian tradition. It dealt with instrumental music in worship. "How can I worship on Sundays when all the worship services provided by the prison use instrumental music in worship?" he asked.

The use of musical instruments in worship has been hotly debated for over a century in the Churches of Christ, who came from a nineteenth-century Christian movement known as the American Restoration Movement. Before the American Civil War, no church within this movement used musical instruments in worship. However, after the war, the richer churches in the North installed organs, which the poorer churches in the South viewed as an unscriptural innovation.

In truth, jealousy and envy were no doubt involved in the conflict, but the official view was that instruments were unscriptural and sparked a controversy that raged for a half-century. Congregations divided over the question, eventually leading to the formation of the non-instrumental Churches of Christ—the part of the movement from which I, and Jeffrey's father, come. We worship *a cappella*—with singing only.

I'd struggled with this question over the years, and finally reached the conclusion that since the Bible is silent on the subject, we have a right, given by God, to praise Him in whatever way we deem best.

So I began, "I appreciate your question, but I think, given your circumstances, you need to be around Christians and all who claim to be Christians more than anything else. So I suggest that you simply attend every chapel and church service you can that is Christian in nature."

"I can't believe you said that!" he exclaimed. "My father is real involved in the Church of Christ, and I know how much worshipping without instruments means to him. How can you say I should worship with every Christian group?"

"Jeff, your greatest need now is for spiritual encouragement. I can't be there every Sunday. The reality of your world is a prison setting. It is far from the ideal circumstances we would like. You need to seek out those who believe many of the same things you believe and worship with them."

"But what about the instrumental music?" he asked.

"I have studied that question a lot, and I have found that the Bible doesn't address the subject at all, at least in terms of the arguments. So, I don't think it matters as much to God as it does to us."

"I can't believe this. What about that passage in Ephesians? Here, I'll read it: 'Speaking to yourselves in psalms and hymns and spiritual songs, singing and making melody in your heart to the Lord.' [Ephesians 5:19]

Doesn't that teach us that singing is the only acceptable way to worship?" he asked.

"What does that passage mean?" I responded. "What is that passage talking about?

"I don't know. You're the expert here! You tell me!" he answered somewhat defensively.

"That passage in Ephesians never mentions anything about musical instruments. That's not the topic Paul is discussing. It's about our lives as Christians—that we should live our lives, day by day, as fully for Jesus as possible.

"My biggest problem with this whole issue," I continued, "is in its approach to the New Testament. To conclude that a passage like this means that we are forbidden to sing with musical accompaniment is to suggest that the New Testament is a law book like the Law of Moses. That is, to violate the law is to put your soul at risk."

"Yes, that is exactly my concern!" he responded.

"But the New Testament is not a law book. It is nothing like the Law of Moses. Just compare the New Testament to the book of Leviticus in the Old Testament. That's a book of law provided by God. Every little detail is given and the correct order is important. But you don't find that in the New Testament. If you realize that the New Testament is not a rulebook, you begin to see it differently. When you read this text in its context, you come away with a completely different understanding.

"Actually, I prefer to sing without an instrument, and that is the true reason I worship the way I do," I said.

Jeff sat there silent for a few minutes, thinking about what I had said. It was obvious I had burst a religious bubble of his, and he needed some time to deal with it.

"This makes sense to me," he finally answered. "But, I will have to think about this for a long time."

"Yes, do that. In the meantime, if you think it would be better for you to worship alone in your cell, go ahead and do that. But, my best advice to you is that you need to associate with other prisoners who claim to be Christian, and who can encourage you, and whom you can encourage."

We didn't talk about this question any more, but I know Jeff took my advice. The question about the Bible translation would return a few times. But over time, week in and week out, Jeff grew to trust me as a true brother in Christ, and I grew to appreciate his desire to learn and to keep himself right with God. Jeff wanted to do the right thing. He had been on the wrong path long enough, and now he wanted to go where God was.

Over the years, people have questioned me about Jeff's sincerity of faith. If they could have looked into his eyes and spoken to his heart, as I did for months, they would understand his great desire to make things right. He had lived wrongly for far too long. For him, every detail mattered greatly. I had to explain the meaning of grace and how it was applied many times before he was able to relax this concern. Once he could see that being a Christian made him right in God's sight, no matter what, he was able to lay aside many of his fears.

CHAPTER 9
ATTACKED

"Dahmer adjusted very well to prison life at the
Columbia Correctional Institute in Portage, Wisconsin.
Initially, he was not part of the general population of the prison,
which would have jeopardized his safety. As it was,
he was attacked on July 3, 1994, while attending a chapel service,
by a Cuban whom he had never seen before....Dahmer,
the model prisoner, [had] convinced the prison authorities
to allow him more contact with other inmates."

COURT TV CRIME LIBRARY,
"JEFFREY DAHMER: END OF THE ROAD"

AS I visited Jeff each week, I saw that my goal of studying the life of Jesus with him would have to be put on hold. During each visit, he brought up another question that bothered him.

His chief concern was that he do the right thing as far as religious practice was concerned. He had plenty of experiences doing wrong things, and now that he was getting right with God, he wanted to make certain that every little detail was proper and correct. Other prison ministers have assured me that this tendency to swing from total lawbreaker to profound law keeper is a normal reaction on the part of many prisoners.

As I've mentioned, when a person in prison finds God, most of what they expect about God is expressed in terms of rule keeping. They have been blatant rule breakers, so their change to an opposite kind of life means they see God as the ultimate rule keeper. The concept is rather simple. Leaving one kind of life for another means a big turnabout—hence keeping the rules instead of breaking them.

Of course, this approach to faith is very legalistic in nature, and I am uncomfortable with a legalistic faith. I come from a legalistic religious background myself, and I am very much aware of its dangers.

Much of my own upbringing focused on law keeping. I was taught to serve God because obedience was commanded, and every aspect of faith was command-oriented. You do only what you are commanded to do, and you dare not go beyond the command. To institute new things is to "innovate." All innovations are sin. The Bible is used to support this approach by emphasizing the scripture that "whosoever shall add" to the commands of scripture will be condemned by God (Revelation 22:18). This principle in the Bible is sound, but its legalistic use fills spiritual life with fear and guilt.

Being raised in legalism, I found that service to God is always suspect. "Have I failed God in some way?" "Will God condemn me because I somehow neglected to cross a 't' or dot an 'i' in my service to him?"

I hoped to spare Jeff from a legalistic faith. I saw my role as a shepherd leading him away from the dangerous swift waters of legalism, and toward the beautiful still waters of grace. Because Jeff's self-esteem was very low, I found myself constantly encouraging him to accept God's love and grace.

"Jeff, you must understand what it means to be a son of God. God looks on you just as he looked on Jesus. Do you remember what God said about Jesus?"

"I don't know what you mean. Are you talking about when Jesus got baptized?" Jeff asked.

"That's one of the times. The other was when Jesus was transfigured on the mountain. God spoke from heaven about Jesus. Do you remember what God said?" I pressed.

"Yes, I do," he replied. "He said, 'This is my beloved Son in whom I am well pleased.'"

"Right. My point is that God thinks of you that way now. When he looks at you, he says, 'This is my beloved son, Jeff, in whom I am well pleased,'" I explained.

"I don't know if I can believe that," he confessed. "I have been so evil and done such bad things, I don't see how he could ever look on me that way."

"But he does, Jeff. It's what's called unconditional love. God loves you without conditions. He loves you for who you are. It doesn't matter what you've done in the past; all that matters is that now you are his child. Everything you do and everything you want to do is to please him. He knows that, and that is why he takes great pleasure in you," I reassured him.

"I just have a hard time believing that," he said.

"Well, you must believe it. You can't earn a better place with God than where you are right now. You don't need to worry about getting everything right. Everything about you is already right, as far as God is concerned, because you are his child."

I emphasized this to Jeff because I'd learned that the real problem with legalism is that your faith shifts subtly to yourself and your ability to "keep the rules" rather than staying focused on Jesus. As long as you think you have kept the rules, then you are all right with God. You start looking at others, and you notice that they don't keep the same rules you do, and you begin to condemn them in your heart. "What kind of a Christian can he be if he doesn't keep the rules?" Before you know it, you start eliminating other people from the pool of Christians you associate with simply because you disagree about the rules. That attitude does nothing but poison your faith. I wanted the best possible faith for Jeff.

On one of our visits, Jeff complained about a problem that had developed and that he didn't know how to deal with. As it turns out, the solution was very simple.

"I get a lot of mail," he began. "Most of it is unsolicited publications, like magazines. I don't mind getting religious materials and letters from people I've never heard of before, but I really don't like getting pornographic material. It always comes in a brown paper wrapping, and everyone knows what it is."

"I know what you mean," I responded. "I sometimes receive the same thing in the mail. I just throw it away."

"Yeah, but you don't understand," he protested. "I used to use that kind of stuff to get myself ready before I committed my crimes. I really don't want to even see that stuff anymore because it reminds me of the kind of man I used to be."

It was clear from the sound of his voice and the expression on his face that receiving the pornography deeply troubled him. He was on the verge of defeat. Here was an area of his life that was still very vulnerable, and he wanted the temptation gone. "What sort of pictures are we talking about?" I asked.

"Oh, you know what I mean, naked women in lewd positions or girls in provocative poses," he replied.

This surprised me. I knew of Jeff's homosexuality. Why did prurient pictures of women—not of men—bother him? Yet, here he was, obviously feeling great spiritual anxiety. What did this mean? Perhaps the point was not whether the pictures were of men or of women, but that they were lewd. I welcomed the fact that he didn't want to go back to those feelings or memories.

"Have you spoken about this to the guards who bring your mail?" I asked. "Have you spoken to the chaplain about this?"

"No," he replied.

"Don't they censor your mail? I'm surprised they would let something like this pass," I exclaimed.

"No, they do that all the time," he said. "They'll open everything else I get in the mail, but this will come unopened."

"Well, I'm really shocked!" I said.

"I'm really bothered by it," he confessed.

"Why don't you explain this to the chaplain or to the prison authorities in charge of your mail, and simply tell them that you don't want to get this kind of stuff. Ask that whenever they see it, to throw it away and not give it to you," I suggested.

"I suppose I could do that," he replied.

And that was that. The subject never came up again. I believe he took my advice.

The prison system and the rules about receiving published materials have always amazed me. An inmate cannot receive a book or a Bible unless it comes from a publishing house. As a visitor, I could not simply give a book to Jeff to read. If he were to have it, I would have to purchase it from a bookstore or a publishing house, and they would have to send it to him. On the other hand, pornographic material can come flying in, and no one bothers to stop it. Where are the priorities and good judgment in this? I don't see much.

On July 4, 1994, Jeff was in the news again. He had attended a church service in the prison chapel on July 3, and as the service concluded, Jeff was attacked. Someone tried to cut his throat. The attacker did not succeed, but only scratched Jeff's neck. I knew we would have some serious things to discuss when I saw him on July 6.

When I arrived for my visit, Chaplain Burkum met me at the prison guard's desk and escorted me to a private consultation room. He wanted to talk with me before I saw Jeff. I immediately wondered if the situation was worse than I thought.

"I want to know if you plan to say anything to the media about Jeff's experience," he began. "We don't want you to speak to the media at all."

"I wasn't planning to say anything to anyone about it," I responded.

"Well, the people who called you about Jeff's baptism didn't throw away your phone number. They will probably call you again to see what your take on this matter is," he explained.

"That's true," I said.

"The prison is very upset about what happened, and I want to assure you that special steps are being taken so that nothing like this will ever happen again," he continued. "Every time the media brings attention to Jeff that just makes it more dangerous for him and harder for us to protect him. You must not say anything to the newspapers, to the radio, to television or to anyone about what happened to Jeff," he emphasized.

"I appreciate the extra steps that are going to be taken to protect Jeff," I told him. "I wouldn't have thought such a thing could happen here, but I'm just glad Jeff wasn't hurt. I don't intend to speak to anyone about it."

At the time, I believed the chaplain's words. He seemed sincerely embarrassed about the whole thing, and it looked as if the prison would not allow anything like this to happen again.

I met Jeff in our usual room, but this time he came with handcuffs and leg irons that had to be removed before he could see me. I wondered why he was being punished for being attacked. Apparently, this is the normal practice in the whole prison system. Anyone who gets in trouble is automatically punished with solitary confinement.

"Man, those handcuffs hurt," Jeff said as he sat down at the table across from me. "You can see the imprint on my wrists." He held out his hands for me to see.

"Why do they have you in handcuffs?" I asked, confused.

"It's the standard prison reaction to what happened. Since I was attacked, both me and the guy who came after me were put in the 'hole,'" Jeff explained. "We'll have to stay there until this is all cleared up. I don't guess that guy will be let out at all."

"Can you tell me what happened?" I asked.

"Sure. I had gone to church in the prison chapel," he explained. "After the service, I remained in my pew a little longer to think about the sermon. Suddenly, I felt a pressure around my neck. Someone had grabbed me and had wrapped their arm under my chin. I began to struggle, and I remember my glasses flying off. As I fell to the floor, I felt my breath being cut off. While we were wrestling around on the floor, he brought his other hand over and dragged something across my neck. You can see the scratch it made!" he said showing me the noticeable red line across his throat.

"What was it he scratched you with?" I probed.

"It was a toothbrush. He had used tape to attach a disposable razor to it, and was trying to cut my throat!" Jeff exclaimed. "But the tape didn't hold, and all he could do was scratch me."

"Did you know him? Why did he want to kill you?" I asked.

"No, I didn't know him. He's a Cuban who was only transferred to my unit a couple of weeks ago," Jeff said. "I have heard that he was really unhappy about being here in prison and was looking for a way to be deported and sent back to Cuba. The best way to do that was to kill someone famous. Since I'm the only famous guy around, that meant he had to kill me in order to go back to Cuba."

This was funny, in a strange sort of way, because in the news at that time were stories of several Cuban families who had made rafts and boats in a frantic effort to come to the United States. "I guess he would be going against traffic to go back to Cuba," I commented. "Poor guy, he doesn't know which way to go!"

"Yeah, I guess so," Jeff joked. I was glad he could laugh about it, but it was clear the experience shook him.

"What do you have to say about all this?" I asked.

"You know, there are times I have longed for death," he confessed. "I really don't want to go on living, at times. But this experience has made me appreciate the life I now have. I am so grateful to God that I have been spared. I praise God that I am alive!"

"You are happy you were not hurt?" I asked.

"Definitely," he responded. "There is so much I want to do for God here in prison, so many people I want to share the gospel with. I want to talk to my mother about my faith. I can't imagine God taking those opportunities away from me now. I am so thankful that I survived."

It was clear to me that Jeff had no death wish. After his death, that question would be put to me several times. Although a part of Jeff wanted to die and go away forever, the man I worked and studied with and came to know was a man who appreciated the life he had left and intended to serve God as much as he could.

"What does this attack mean in terms of the other prisoners you have to associate with?" I asked. "Does this mean there are others who may want to kill you?"

"I don't think so," he replied. "Generally, I get along well with the other prisoners. They respect me and I respect them. Of course, you can't allow someone to take advantage of you; that's another matter altogether. No, I'd say I get along real well with the other guys in here. I don't see any of them hating me or trying to make my life harder."

I was comforted by these words. After Jeff's murder months later at the hands of another inmate, those words would come back to haunt me, but at the time, I believed him. I felt, from what the prison chaplain had said and from what Jeff had said, that he would be safe. He had many enemies outside the prison, but he didn't know of any within it.

Jeff then made a suggestion that caught me off guard. He said he thought my visits were a hardship on me and on my family.

"You know, you don't have to come see me every week. If you want to stop coming, that would be all right," he said.

"What are you talking about?" I asked.

"Well, I know it takes time for you to come see me, time you could be spending with your family," he began. "I know it has to cost you some money to make the trip every week to see me. I was just saying that you don't have to go to all that trouble just for me."

"Look," I replied, "I spend plenty of time with my family, and the money it takes to come see you is well within my means. I consider it a privilege to come see you as often as I do, and I intend to keep coming, unless you don't want me to come."

"Oh no, that's not what I'm saying," he replied. "It's just that I really appreciate all you've done, but I don't want you to think that you have to come see me."

"Well, as it turns out," I began, "I do have to take a short vacation from seeing you this summer. I work in a summer youth camp associated with my church work. I'll be working in the middle of July with kids from ages 13 to 15. But that is the only time I plan to be gone. I intend to keep coming to see you after my camp session is done."

"How long will you be gone?" he asked.

"Just two weeks," I answered. "I imagine growing old along with you. I can see us as two old men, studying the Bible together every week, as we are now. I can imagine our doing this until either of us dies." I didn't realize how true my words would be.

"Well," he said, "I just don't want to be a problem for you."

"Don't worry," I replied, "you're no problem at all." It was important for me to affirm his place in my life. I intended to have a place in my heart for Jeff for a long, long time.

CHAPTER 10
THE LETTER

"Now, many months after Jeff's trial and our ordeal, I remain a man in constant rumination, often tortured in soul by the deeds of my offspring. I find that I remain in the grip of a great unknowing, both in terms of Jeff himself, and my effect upon him as a father, by omissions and commissions. Fatherhood remains, at last, a grave enigma, and when I contemplate that my other son may one day be a father, I can only say to him, as I must to every father after me, 'Take care, take care, take care.'"

LIONEL DAHMER, *A FATHER'S STORY*, 1994

WHEN summer comes to Wisconsin, it brings special responsibilities because so much more is going on than in the winter. The winters are harsh in Wisconsin, and the summers are highly valued as times to be outdoors.

If you plan many meetings during the summer months you won't have much participation. Everyone is out hiking, camping, boating, gardening or on vacation. For me, summer is always dominated by my work at a Christian Bible camp.

This particular year, I was a director of the Intermediate Camp at Fallhall Glen, a camp just south of Black River Falls, Wisconsin. The campers were early high school students. Wisconsin Christian Youth Camp, the camp association, does not employ any of the staff; all the workers are volunteers. That meant that I had to recruit the adult participants—cooks, cabin counselors, Bible teachers, lifeguards, a nurse, a crafts teacher and a nature leader. Trying to convince people to take time off from their jobs to work with adolescent children for free is quite a task. It takes many phone calls, letters, begging and persuasion. The whole process is time-consuming and sometimes overwhelming.

Despite that, I was able to keep my regular weekly visits with Jeff up until July 13 before the camp session began on July 17. I had explained to Jeff that I wouldn't see him for two weeks. The schedule at camp leaves no time to think about anyone or anything else, and I'd said I would return to my regular visits after camp was over. My announcement that I'd be gone two weeks did come when he said I didn't need to continue visiting him. But I thought I'd been perfectly clear that I did not intend to stop my visits.

The camp session went well with relatively few problems, and I was focused on my work and on the needs of the children and the staff. I did not think about Jeff at all until I received a letter in the mail. It was from my wife, Susan, and included a letter from Lionel Dahmer, Jeff's father. It was quite a surprise, although I had hoped to talk with Mr. Dahmer at some point.

A part of me identified with Lionel Dahmer. We were both Christian parents. My son had been in some trouble with the police, too, on lesser offenses. My son once spent time in jail for his failure to pay fines for reckless driving, and then for driving with a revoked license. I remember how embarrassed I was as a Christian, yet how torn I felt as a parent. Even though he deserved punishment from the state of Wisconsin, I still loved my son and wanted the best for him.

I have a vivid memory of making a trip to the jail to take my son his glasses so he could take out his contacts, and having a hard time getting his contacts back from an uncooperative jail guard. My treatment by the guards as the father of a person in jail burned into my psyche. Although my experience with my son was minor in comparison to Lionel Dahmer's, I planned to tell him, as best as I could, that I understood something of what he felt.

When I read his letter, I was immediately concerned. Lionel had the idea from something Jeff had written that I planned to stop my visits. Perhaps Jeff had written him this before my last visit with him—or perhaps Jeff had not believed the assurances of my commitment to continue my visits.

Lionel wrote, "I really appreciate the time and expense you have taken to minister to Jeff. I realize it takes time away from your family and other activities to visit him, as well as financial expense to drive to the prison." This sounded just like what Jeff had said at our last visit.

He continued, "Jeff mentioned that your visits will cease in the near future. Since Jeff is a new Christian convert, it is very important that he have follow-up support visits. I am limited to occasional visits, phone calls and letters to Jeff, which really is not enough. The personal contact and study on a regular basis is what will keep him going. I have seen him become enthusiastic about other things, only to drop his enthusiasm after a time. I think that he is very sincere and well-grounded for starters."

Lionel had the same idea I had about what Jeff needed, but gave an interesting insight. He feared he would treat this "Christian" thing like he'd treated many other things in his life. He'd be excited about it for a time, but eventually would give it up. Lionel Dahmer was worried about his son.

He said, "Is there any person or group who could possibly continue visitation, study and worship with Jeff, at least until Jeff is really well grounded in his faith? I know I'm asking a lot of strangers to do this for me."

His letter concluded, "I think it is especially important to continue follow-up, because Jeff is very dedicated at the moment. He has even put study pamphlets in the prison chapel for other inmates to see."

Lionel didn't have to convince me of the importance of developing Jeff's faith. In my visits with him, I had seen Jeff's desire to "spread the word" among other inmates.

When Susan read Lionel's letter, she immediately called him. Lionel had included a business card with his phone numbers. They had a good, long conversation about Jeff and about his faith, and she was able to reassure him that I would never desert Jeff.

Lionel's letter had an interesting postscript: "Please do not mention to Jeff that I have pleaded with you to help me attain continued follow-up, as he has a mind of his own. I wouldn't want him to feel I am 'arranging' things for him."

By this time, I had read Lionel's book about Jeff, *A Father's Story*. In it, he didn't reveal much understanding of the Jeff I knew, but he revealed much about his relationship with Jeff. Their relationship had always been distant, and Lionel generally kept his distance from Jeff emotionally—although he loved him deeply.

As a young man, Jeff was incredibly passive about his future. When he and his father made contact, it was usually for Lionel to tell Jeff what he

PHOTO: ASSOCIATED PRESS

SHARI AND LIONEL DAHMER AT JEFFREY DAHMER'S TRIAL

thought he should do with his life. And I knew, as a father who also loved his son and found himself in a disapproving role, that these confrontations do not go well for either father or son.

After his divorce and after Jeff graduated from high school, Lionel told Jeff to go to the University of Ohio, and he obeyed. Jeff's alcoholism and irresponsibility got him kicked out of the University in a short time. Lionel then told him to join the United States Army. Again, Jeff offered little argument. He joined and was eventually discharged for his alcoholism. Lionel sent Jeff to live with his grandmother, Lionel's mother, and later after the grandmother's complaints about Jeff, told him to move into his own apartment.

I wanted to talk with Lionel father to father. I had learned lessons with my son that I hoped to share. I had wanted to make up for lost time and lost ground with my own son, but came to realize that a time comes when it is too late. The best I could do was just love my son, regardless. I think that's where Lionel was.

Throughout the world, Lionel's family name, "Dahmer," now conjures up images of horror and depravity. Many a father faced with such infamy and with the immensity of these crimes would have abandoned his son, changed his name and left the country. I admired Lionel for his faithfulness.

After the camp session, I wrote him:

Dear Brother Lionel,

I was very happy to receive your letter. It came while I was directing a two-week session at a Christian summer camp, so I was not able to answer immediately. I felt it would be inappropriate for me to try to contact you on my own. I imagined that you were troubled enough with people trying to contact you about Jeff, and my fears were confirmed somewhat in a conversation with Bruce Gleim. When your letter arrived, I was greatly overjoyed!

I had spoken with Lionel's minister, Bruce Gleim, after Jeff's baptism. He left the impression that Lionel was hounded by the press and did not want to be bothered by anyone. I had asked him to encourage Lionel to contact me. I continued,

> I wanted to communicate with you as a fellow father. My son has been in trouble with the police also. Although my experience is nothing comparable to yours, a part of me connects with what I imagine you are going through. I wanted to give you some comfort and try to ease your mind of the anxieties you may have.
>
> I know that you and my wife had a great conversation. Although she told you this, let me reiterate that I am totally committed to Jeff. It was his idea that the time, travel and expense were too much for me. He said he would understand if I wanted to end our meetings. I had no such thought. As far as I am concerned, he's stuck with me! I don't intend to quit until either he refuses to meet with me, or the Lord sends me away.
>
> If I should have to move, I would make arrangements for someone else to continue to meet with him until he feels there is no longer a need. Sometimes, when Jeff gets a thought in his mind, it is very difficult to get it corrected or changed! I do not intend to end my visits with him.

I wanted Lionel to know that I had worked enough with Jeff to understand some of his quirks, particularly his ability to set his mind on something and not let go. I had seen this in some of our discussions regarding the Bible translations and other issues. Once he had his mind made up, he didn't like to change it. I continued,

> Obviously, Jeff is not in an ideal circumstance to build a strong Christian faith, but we are doing the best we can. Jeff has been somewhat evangelistic in his desire to share the gospel with other inmates. He takes the Lord's Supper every Sunday in his cell, unless it is offered in the prison chapel. By the way, that was his idea, which I thought was excellent.
>
> Jeff asks questions and listens when I open the Bible to show him what I understand the Scriptures to say on many subjects. He is very much like a sponge, trying to absorb as much as he possibly can. He wants to get his life right in every detail.

I tried to reassure Lionel about Jeff's safety.

> Judging from the reaction of the prison chaplain and the guards to the attempt on Jeffrey's life, I believe the chapel is more secure now than it has been in the past. I don't have as much reservation about it as I did before.
>
> I want to tell you that Jeffrey's respect for you is profound. He regards your opinions as almost holy. His love for you and your wife, Shari, goes very deep. As you mentioned, he is his own man; and I know he probably would resent any effort on your part to arrange things for him. But I felt you needed to know how highly he regards the both of you.

I hope we can keep in touch. My wife mentioned that you would like to meet us sometime. That would be great. I'll close with a comment about your son by a prison guard on my last visit. He said, 'In spite of what he did, he is really a decent guy.' I told him I thought so, too.

God bless you,

Roy Ratcliff

Lionel never answered this letter or contacted me. The next time I heard from him was after Jeff's death. I had hoped to have a closer relationship with this man because we had a common concern for Jeff. Lionel had to walk his own, very difficult path.

When Lionel and I finally did meet to plan Jeff's memorial service, I told him more of my perceptions about Jeff, as well as things I had discussed with Jeff that I think he would have wanted to discuss with his father.

My heart goes out for Lionel Dahmer. I knew his son, and I knew his role as a father. I admired him for his courage and support of his son, despite the world's hatred. I respected him for his efforts to make up for lost ground. I saw him make great effort to overcome his mistakes as a father.

But my work was to be with his son. Jeff was the one I had to focus upon and help develop his faith. My heart went out to his father, but it was the son to whom I was sent. I would discover he was a normal human being, and that I liked him. The son became my friend.

CHAPTER 11
FRIENDSHIP

"It was the Wednesday before Thanksgiving Day, 1994.

On that day, Jeff gave me the card, and below its Thanksgiving

message he had written: 'Dear Roy, Thank you for your friendship....'

That card is one of my most precious possessions. It is precious

because it came from a friend who was willing

to express the feelings of his heart."

ROY RATCLIFF

AFTER Jeff's death, I was interviewed once again by many people from television, radio, magazines and newspapers. They all seemed to have the same questions and concerns, and I was often asked how I felt about Jeff personally.

I told them I felt I had become his friend, and he had become my friend. I remember that one comedian picked up on that and built a routine around it. I guess he found it incredible that I—or anyone—could have a friendship with someone like Jeffrey Dahmer.

The comedian ended his routine with a twist on the advertisement against drunk driving, and said, "Friends don't let friends eat friends." Most people cannot get past the horror of Jeff's crimes; it's all they see. To them, a friendship with Jeffrey Dahmer seemed unthinkable—even comical.

Yet, Jeff and I did develop a good relationship. Week after week, I visited him, and we talked about whatever was on his mind. Eventually, we began to study the Bible together to answer his questions about the meaning of life and faith in God.

Jeff wanted to study the book of Revelation and the apocalypse—the end of time, so I chose the book of Hebrews to study first as an introduction to Revelation. "Hebrews has keys that unlock the mysterious doors of Revelation," I told him.

What Jeff didn't understand was that Revelation, as well as Hebrews, is not so much about the end of the world as it is about faith. Its theme and purpose is to encourage people to hang onto their faith, no matter what happens or how dire their circumstances seem. I knew Jeff needed this message.

"The most important thing in life, Jeff, is to have faith," I would tell him. "There are all kinds of terrible circumstances which, I think, God sends us, that demand we believe on him and follow through with that belief."

"I can see that in my own life," Jeff replied. "Although it took bad things to bring me to the position I'm in, I don't think I would have any kind of faith in God without them."

"Yes," I said, "it is amazing how God can use the bad things in our lives to bring about the good things he wants to bless us with."

I have often counseled marriage partners to just talk with each other in intimate ways in the belief that such close, personal talk will produce trust. Trust is the single most important element necessary in maintaining a healthy marriage or a friendship. It is a window into another's heart. Jesus talked about this in Matthew when describing that people are either good or evil. He said, "For out of the overflow of the heart the mouth speaks" (Matthew 12:34).

Each week, as Jeff and I would talk about what we had studied, and about what was going on in his life, I could see his heart opening up to me.

"I want to do what's right and think what's right," Jeff confessed, "but sometimes it's so hard because of the people I have to deal with."

"I know what you mean," I said. "I have no idea what it's like in prison, of course, other than from my visits with you, but I know people are still people, no matter where you are. I can imagine you have all kinds of people to deal with who make life hard for you."

"Yeah," he continued, "I generally get along fine with most people, but every now and then you come across someone who is a real jerk about things, and it tries your faith."

"That's why we have to keep believing and not give up," I explained. "God knows our circumstance, and he can give us the strength we need to deal with anyone who comes our way."

One habit we developed as we got into the study of the Bible was to end our meetings in prayer. Prayer is a vital part of faith, and as an older Christian mentoring a younger Christian, it was important to me that Jeff hear my prayers on his behalf. It was also important for me to hear his prayers.

"We need to take turns praying," I told Jeff. "I'll start off with the first prayer, but next week, I would like to have you say the closing prayer." He looked a little bewildered and uncertain. "You need to do this," I continued, "because you need to learn how to pray and how to feel more comfortable praying. The more I hear you, the more I'm able to coach you on how to improve your prayers."

"Okay, if you'll coach me along, I'll give it a try," he said.

When the next week came around, Jeff prayed his first prayer between us. "Father in heaven, thank you for sending Roy into my life, and having him help me to better understand your words and your ways," he began. There were periods of pauses when he had to think about what he wanted to say, and he did it haltingly, but he managed to get good words out. "And please bless my dad and his wife, and my mom too," he continued. "Help me to be a better person. Amen."

"That was good, Jeff," I said. "Your concerns were from the heart and that's what matters to God."

As the weeks passed, we developed the habit of talking briefly about the concerns that needed to be included in our prayers. Jeff's always involved his family—his father and stepmother and especially his mother. Jeff rarely spoke of his younger brother, David. They were about six years apart in age, and it was obvious there was little relationship between them. But he cared deeply about his mother and his father.

"My mother has got some kind of weird belief that God is in the trees and in the winds and in animals and things. I really wish she could come back to her faith," Jeff said. "Well, we will pray for her and for her faith too," I replied. "I know you love her and care for her."

"Yeah, I'm trying to make an arrangement with a publishing house to ship her some of the materials my Dad has sent me," he continued.

"What sort of materials?" I asked.

"Oh, about the creation of the world and how evolution is untrue. That's where I got my faith in God, from those materials, and I just know if she would look at them, she could get her faith back too," he explained.

"Well, it doesn't always work that way, Jeff," I answered, "but I'll pray for her too. Who knows what God can do?"

When you pray with someone about his family, and he lets you into his life and allows you to see his concerns and feel his worries, you get closer to his heart. You begin to feel friendship.

One of the issues that bothered Jeff most was his responsibility toward the families of his victims. Everything he owned had been taken away from him, and there was nothing else he could do for them. He felt very bad about the pain and suffering he had brought them, but what more could he do than what he had done during his trial? But there was a lawyer who represented several of the families, and had made it his goal in life to make Jeff pay.

"This lawyer for the families of my victims came here under false pretenses," Jeff explained. "He was supposed to be working on another case, but while he was here, he pulled out my file and learned that I had a job in prison. I make a whopping 25 cents an hour for cleaning out the bathroom. Well, this guy went and filed a motion with a judge to freeze my canteen account so that my measly 25 cents an hour would be given to the families of my victims," he complained.

"Why is this a problem?" I asked.

"Because it doesn't allow me to do anything for myself, such as buy postage stamps, coffee or cigarettes from the canteen," he answered. "I haven't had a cup of coffee or a cigarette for so long, I can't stand it!" he said, his voice rising. "I can't even write a letter!"

"I see what you mean," I replied.

"I feel bad for the families of my victims, but my 25 cents an hour divided among them is nothing. But that same 25 cents makes life more bearable for me," he said. "I can live being uncomfortable about my crimes, but this is ridiculous!"

I could see how the lawyer could feel this was a symbolic act of justice. On the other hand, Jeff was paying for his crimes by being in prison. Is the point of prison to torment him over and over again? I felt for him, and I felt for his anguish, too.

Over the weeks, our friendship grew. I looked forward to my weekly trip to see him, and I thought of things to talk about when we weren't studying the Bible. Our visits had become a highlight of my regular weekly duties.

But did Jeff consider me a friend? I think the answer is in a Thanksgiving card he gave me on my last visit. I did not know, of course, nor did he, that it would be my last visit. It was the Wednesday before Thanksgiving Day, 1994.

On that day, Jeff gave me the card, and below its Thanksgiving message he had written: "Dear Roy, Thank you for your friendship, and for taking the time and effort to help me understand God's word. God bless you and your family! Sincerely, Jeff Dahmer." That card is one of my most precious possessions. It is precious because it came from a friend who was willing to express the feelings of his heart.

Jeffrey Dahmer was my friend.

CHAPTER 12

JOURNEY'S END

"So who was Jeffrey Dahmer? We must admit

immediately that no one will ever know,

that Jeffrey is a mystery even to himself....

No book can claim to have discovered

the ultimate solution to the enigma...."

THOMAS H. COOK,

FOREWORD, *A FATHER'S STORY*, 1994

I WILL never forget November 28, 1994. It was Monday morning, my day off. Susan and I were driving home from the gym, passing the time in small talk, including things I intended to mention to Jeff when I would see him on Wednesday.

"I want to tell him how our Thanksgiving Day went and how much I appreciated the card he gave me. It will probably be one of my most treasured possessions," I said. Just as we were approaching home, I heard something on the radio about Jeffrey Dahmer. I quickly turned up the volume to hear the news bulletin. The announcer said that Jeff had been attacked and was taken to the hospital with massive head injuries. "What's happened to Jeff?" I exclaimed. Those words were barely out of my mouth when the newsflash was updated: Jeffrey Dahmer was dead.

Jeff had been assigned to clean a bathroom facility in a recreational area at the prison. He wasn't alone. Two other inmates were working with him. One of them, Christopher J. Scarver, went to the weight-lifting machines in the gym and removed a weighted bar. He came up behind Jeff while he was cleaning a bathroom and struck him in the head. He beat him repeatedly until

Jeff fell to the floor unconscious. Then he went after the other inmate, Jesse Anderson, and attacked him too. Mr. Anderson was in a coma for a few days, and then died of his injuries. No one was ever able to establish a motive for Scarver's attack. Although many people on the radio and in the newspapers made speculations—including racial revenge, bribery, drug deals and mental illness—as far as I know, it was never clear why the attack occurred.

I was in a hurry to learn more about Jeff's death. It did not occur to me that the media, who was hungry about Jeff's baptism, would want to know what I thought about his death, as well. When I entered the house, I saw the answering machine blinking. It held several calls, and the phone was ringing again. It was difficult to know what to say. I was as shocked as everyone else. I was stricken with grief. I don't know why I'd never thought this would happen.

Listening to the messages was hard as each one was interrupted by another phone call. Each caller wanted to set up an appointment to interview me. I had to change my clothes quickly and run to my office where the interviews would take place.

I was in a state of shock and denial, hoping against all hope that this was an awful mistake. I had no time to deal with my own feelings. *People* magazine took a picture of me that day, holding up the Thanksgiving Day card Jeff had given me only a few days before. The picture showed how tired and weary I felt. I thought the media attention over Jeff's baptism was rough. This was worse.

In the frenzy of the media coverage, I also received phone calls, cards, and letters from people expressing sympathy for my loss. Many made positive comments about my baptizing Jeff, and how I had ministered to him. No one said anything derogatory or critical of my relationship with him.

However, among those who contacted me were women who had gotten to know Jeff through the mail. He had expressed great appreciation to each of them for showing an interest in him. Apparently, he used words that were easily misinterpreted, for some of these women were convinced they were in love with Jeff, and he was in love with them. I heard from six women, and I think there were at least that many more I never heard from.

One woman made an appointment for counseling for her grief about Jeff, and while we were talking, I received a phone call from another woman several states away, crying about the same thing. It was strange. Some of the women were angry and jealous when they learned through the media that Jeff had sent them all the same poems he had written and used the same language in his letters that conveyed great feeling for them. Most of them thought Jeff was in love with them, and a couple believed they were going to marry him. I knew nothing about these relationships, yet I was asked to explain what Jeff meant when he spoke to each woman of his love and appreciation. I was in an unforeseen and painful situation. I will never know why Jeff developed these relationships, and how they fit into the puzzle of Jeffrey Dahmer.

I received one phone call I had expected. Jeff's father Lionel called to say he was coming to identify Jeff's body and prepare for closing his estate. Jeff had requested cremation and wanted no funeral service. We agreed to meet at Lionel's motel room to discuss my experiences with Jeff and to help him and his wife cope with their grief. He also wanted my help in planning a memorial service.

Susan and I met Lionel and Shari Dahmer at their room and tried to overcome the situation's initial awkwardness. "It is good meeting you, although I wish the circumstances were better," I began. Susan had spoken with Lionel over the phone after he'd written his letter asking me not to forsake Jeff, but I had never spoken to him or met him.

"We saw Jeff today," Lionel began. "One side of his face was bashed in. But what hurt me the most was that he was handcuffed. Can you imagine that? He's lying there dead, and they've still got to handcuff him, as if he were still a threat to someone!" I learned years later of the common prison policy to handcuff every inmate when they are out of the prison facility, regardless. But I didn't know that then.

"I'm shocked. Why would they handcuff him now?" I asked. I identified with Lionel's feelings.

We began to talk about Jeff and about Lionel's role as his father. We talked about three hours. I could identify with Lionel on many things, and I tried to share experiences about Jeff that related to his father.

"Jeff said that you used to take him to church when he was a little boy," I said.

"Yes, that's true," Lionel responded.

"He never understood why you stopped going to church."

"Well, his mother and I were going through some really hard times then," Lionel began. "I think she was manic-depressive. Anyway, she stopped going to church, but I kept on going, taking Jeff with me. The last time I went with Jeff, his mother and I had a horrible fight when I got home. She thought I was trying to make her feel guilty for not going to church. It was so bad that I never wanted to experience that again. So I decided to stay at home, read the Bible and worship God in private," he explained.

"Jeff never understood why you stopped going," I responded.

"I know. I always meant to talk with him about that, but somehow we never got on that subject," he said.

"Jeff had a great deal of love and admiration for you," I told Lionel. "I don't know if you understand how much he loved you, and your ex-wife."

"Yes, I don't think he ever got over our divorce," Lionel replied.

I wanted to pass on to Lionel something Jeff had told me about his faith. "Jeff told me that his journey of faith began with some material you had sent him. He said he did not believe in God until he went through those materials. He credits you with giving him his Christian faith," I told him.

Lionel was shocked. "I've never heard that," he replied. "I always wondered why he wanted to be baptized and when he started believing in God. I remember sending him those materials and hoping they would do some good, but I never heard back from him about them, so I just thought he threw them away," Lionel said.

"Why did you send those materials to him?" I asked. "Why did you start going back to church?"

"Well, it is because of our younger son, David. He went to the University of Ohio and while there, got connected to a Christian student center. David became a Christian and when he came home, he urged me to go back to church. I'm just overwhelmed to find this out about Jeff. This is wonderful news for me!" Lionel said.

We talked also about the memorial service. Lionel wondered if such a thing was appropriate. "I think it is," I answered, "because Jeff still has people who love him and who cared for him. The service is not for him, but for you and for others who cared about him."

Shari Dahmer made a remark that stuck in my mind. "I think Jeff didn't want a funeral or a grave marker because he hated his notoriety so much. I think he wanted to disappear and be forgotten and never be heard of or remembered again." I agreed with her. I know Jeff hated being infamous. He was tired of being hated. For him, death would be sweet in the sense that he would no longer have to deal with people. But his desire was unrealistic. People would not easily forget Jeffrey Dahmer.

Lionel gave me strict instructions. "We would like to use your church building. Don't tell anyone about the memorial service, especially the media. We have two camera crews we trust who will be there. I don't want any local media involved at all," he explained.

"Okay," I replied and looked at him questioningly.

Lionel continued, "You see, our younger son, David, plans to be there and he does not want to be photographed. He has changed his last name, legally, to disassociate himself from his brother, and he does not want to be recognized on camera."

"I understand," I said. "I won't say a thing." Later, after the service was over, I received an angry phone call from one of the local television stations. They felt I had betrayed them. I had to explain that this was the wish of the family.

"Do you expect a small crowd?" I asked.

"I would like for you to invite no more than six families from your congregation to attend the service," Lionel said. "They must be people you feel confident can keep a secret. Under no circumstances is the word to leak out."

Who could I invite? I could come up with six names easily enough, but what about those who were not invited? Would they feel slighted? I would have to use my best judgment, and explain to the rest that Jeff's family requested this, too.

It was late when we finally got home. I still had phone calls to make, and I hoped the people I had to call would understand. Each family felt honored to be invited to the service and swore to keep the service secret.

Before I went to bed, I tried to put together a few thoughts for the memorial. Certain words and phrases in the Bible speak of a Christian's view of death. Paul's words in Philippians seemed especially relevant to me. "To live is Christ, and to die is gain," and "To depart and be with Christ...is better by far" (Philippians 1:21, 23).

Although death is our enemy and is something we dread and fear, the Christian can look at death and not be afraid. For Christians, death can be sweet, for it takes us to live with Christ. Christ is the center of a Christian's life, and any time with him is the best time. Jeff was now with Christ. Some unbelievers will claim Jeff is burning in hell, but we who believe know better.

Finally, I went to sleep, exhausted and numb. Tomorrow we would remember a man most people would rather forget.

CHAPTER 13
THE MEMORIAL

"We are here to remember Jeff and how much we loved him.

That is not to say that those of you here who have suffered

at Jeff's hands are not to be remembered, too. We do not justify

or make light of any of Jeff's crimes. Our hearts go out to you

who have been hurt by Jeff. We mourn with you, and we cry

with you, for those were terrible things Jeff did."

LIONEL DAHMER AT HIS SON'S MEMORIAL SERVICE

JEFF'S memorial service was set for Friday, December 2, 1994.

Lionel had asked me to arrange for a place for his second son, David, to stay. I was planning to ask someone from the church, when Lionel approached me. "There's been a change of plans," he began.

"What do you mean?" I asked.

"David won't be alone. He has some friends with him from the church where he worships, and they would rather stay in a motel than in a home," he explained.

"That's no problem at all, but I thought he was coming alone and needed a place to stay," I said.

"That's what I thought, too," Lionel said. "You see, the relationship between David and me is not the best. There are strained feelings that have not been resolved." He was embarrassed that his effort to take care of his son had failed. He seemed to be a man who had let much time pass without reconnecting, and now was trying to cover much ground too soon. He was doing the best he could.

The church people I had invited arrived and took their places in the pews. A few flowers were at the front, but nothing like what is typical for funerals. The memorial service was very plain and unadorned.

In the audience was someone I didn't expect—a woman who had grown close to Lionel and Shari Dahmer despite every reason to avoid them. She was a sister of one of Jeff's victims. Lionel and Shari had invited her to attend Jeff's memorial. I was only beginning to absorb the irony of that relationship when she introduced me to her sister. She had brought her sister with her, but had not told her what the occasion was. She knew her sister was still bitter and angry about their brother's death, and the way Jeff had killed him.

Apparently, she had found some healing through her association with Lionel and Shari, and she wanted her sister to be healed as well. I could see clearly that the woman was in a state of shock over her sister's deception. She was twisting a tissue in her hands and dabbing periodically at tears running down her cheeks. She constantly looked around for a way of escape. But she was in a situation she couldn't escape, so she took a pew by herself in the back of the church. She stayed there throughout the service and wept silently. My heart went out to her, but I had other duties to perform, and I could not help her.

I asked one of the men from the church to lead some congregational songs. We sang, "Why Did My Savior Come to Earth?" and "The Old Rugged Cross." Afterwards, I stood up and began to speak.

"We are here for a memorial service on behalf of Jeffrey Dahmer. Many of the people here did not know Jeffrey, but have come by invitation to offer comfort to those who knew Jeff and loved him. In the Bible, God is described as the God of all comfort who is able to comfort us when we need it. We are then capable of comforting others. I hope that in this service God's comfort will be felt by all those in need of it. One way we find comfort is by remembering fond memories of the life that was lived. We are going to ask those in the audience who would like to share some of their thoughts and memories of Jeff to speak them now." Then I sat down and waited.

Lionel was the first to stand. "I want you to know that despite the terrible things Jeff did, he was my son, and I loved him very much. I have so many good memories of Jeff as a little boy. He brought so much happiness to our house, and we felt blessed to have him as our son. Some of my fondest memories are when I was trying to teach him how to play tennis. I felt we grew very close to each other then." Lionel continued on for a while recounting his memories as a father.

Lionel paused to look at the sister of Jeff's victim and the other sister sitting at the back of the church. "We are here to remember Jeff and how much we loved him. That is not to say that those of you here who have suffered at Jeff's hands are not to be remembered, too. We do not justify or make light of any of Jeff's crimes. Our hearts go out to you who have been hurt by Jeff. We mourn with you, and we cry with you, for those were terrible things Jeff did. We know you understand the feeling of losing a loved one, and we hope you can join us in our sorrow and loss over Jeff."

Then Lionel spoke about Jeff's faith. "Roy told me just last night that Jeff claimed I led him to his faith in Christ. I am humbled to hear those words and to realize what influence I've had on my son. I did not know he credited me with giving him his faith. I have made many mistakes in my life, and one of the greatest was trying to live the Christian life without the church. I have finally learned that I cannot do it alone. I need others to encourage me and to strengthen me. I would encourage everyone here tonight to heed the lesson I have learned so painfully. God help me, I intend never to abandon my church or my faith again."

After he sat down, there was an awkward silence. I imagine the people were a little stunned by Lionel's strong message. Then David came to the front to speak. I was curious about what he would have to say about his brother, since Jeff hardly spoke of him. But it became clear, very quickly, that David had nothing to say about Jeff either. "I have fond memories too, especially of those days on the tennis courts when Dad was teaching me how to play and later coaching me," he began.

The rest of his words became a blur to me as I realized he was not speaking about Jeff at all. He was trying desperately to connect with his father, and he was using this occasion, whether appropriate or not, to do it. All of his memories were about himself and his father. Not a word was said of his brother. What kind of relationship, if any, existed between the brothers? I remembered that David had his last name changed legally to distance himself from his brother. Was he here just to see his father? Did he care about his brother at all?

After David sat down, one of his friends stood up to speak. I wondered if he knew Jeff. He spoke in grand generalities about the pain of death and the hope of salvation that every Christian embraces. He emphasized that Jesus does understand our feelings. What he had to say was fine, but it had nothing to do with Jeffrey Dahmer.

His words could have been my words at the funeral of a person I'd never met. Most of the funerals I've conducted in my ministry career have been for people I've never met. I know how easy it is to speak in grand generalities about life and death and hope someone is listening, when few are. What a strange experience. We were at a memorial service, and two of the three speakers never said a word about the deceased.

After David's friend sat down, another period of silence followed. I was waiting to see if anyone else wanted to speak about Jeff. When I was assured no one else did, I returned to the podium for some closing words.

"Every life is important. Some would mock us for gathering here to remember a life that has caused so much hurt. But we come to focus not on the crimes he committed, but on the faith that changed his life. I know Jeff believed in God and trusted Christ to save him. I baptized him, studied with him, and got to know his heart. He was truly sorry for the things he had done.

"Many people were shocked and scandalized by his baptism," I continued, "but I think their shock is really anger. They cannot conceive that anyone who committed Jeff's terrible crimes could come to Christ. If he did, indeed, come to Christ, they would rather Christ turn his face away and reject him. But they did not understand why Jesus came to earth. He came to save sinners. Jeff was a sinner.

"Their anger is illustrated by a story in a book by Max Lucado called *Six Hours One Friday*.

Once a Bible school teacher had a little girl in class who never spoke. Week after week, lesson after lesson, no matter what others said or did, this little girl was absolutely quiet. The teacher began to wonder what kind of home she must have come from that taught her to be so still.

Then one day, the teacher was teaching a lesson about heaven.

She tried to paint the most vivid pictures of golden streets and a beautiful river flowing through it, with wonderful trees on the riverbank that produced fruit that would heal you. She noticed, as she was teaching the lesson, that this particular little girl was focused on her every word.

At the end of the class, the little girl held up her hand as if to ask a question. This was a momentous occasion. Was the little girl who never spoke going to ask a question? The teacher called on the girl and the girl did speak, but her question was piercing. She asked, 'Is heaven for little girls like me?'

"I am struck by that question. My experience with Jeff reminds me of that story—only Jeff is the little child. Instead of being in the class, I imagine him outside, looking through a window. In the end, he is asking the same question, 'Is heaven for boys like me? I've been terribly bad. Could I possibly go to heaven, too?' You see, the answer for both the little girl and for Jeff is the same: Yes, heaven is for people just like you."

I saw I had the attention of the deceived sister in the back of the church. She was still crying, but she was staring hard at me. "Jeff confessed to me his great remorse for his crimes. He wished he could do something for the families of his victims to make it right, but there was nothing he could do. He turned to God because there was no one else to turn to, but he showed great courage in his daring to ask the question, 'Is heaven for me, too?' I think many people are resentful of him for asking that question. But he dared to ask, and he dared to believe the answer."

Then I spoke directly to the two sisters of one of Jeff's victims. "We strongly sympathize with those of you who have been hurt by Jeff's criminal activities. We share in your sorrow, too. Although we are involved in a memorial for Jeff, I want you to know that we care about your feelings, too. The thing we are remembering here is that Jeff turned to God for forgiveness, and God is willing to forgive someone as bad as Jeff. I believe if Jeff were here right now, he would look at you and apologize for what he did to your brother. He was a changed man. He was being remade into the image of Jesus Christ."

We ended the service with a prayer and stayed to visit with one another. I went back to speak to the sister in the back pew. "I appreciate your being here, despite the fact that I understand you were deceived into coming," I said.

She said, "Yes, I was upset when I first got here because I was still bitter about Jeffrey Dahmer, and I had not forgiven him. But hearing you describe him as you knew him has helped me. I believe God has forgiven him, and I can forgive him and move on with my life."

"May God bless you and comfort you in your loss. I'm deeply touched by your words," I said.

Afterwards, Shari Dahmer gave me an honorarium for conducting the service. This was unexpected, but was graciously received. Susan and I took the money and bought an expensive wall clock for our living room. We call it Jeff's clock. It reminds us of the lessons I learned from my experiences with Jeff, and of the value of time well spent.

I was deeply shocked by Jeff's death. I had anticipated visiting him and studying with him for many years. That I was given only seven months to work with him was inconceivable to me. I was forced to ask myself if I had prepared him to meet his God. The clock reminds me to use my time wisely, for time passes quickly. In the end, I believe I did prepare him for his death. He was ready to die. I was the one who was unprepared.

About a week after the memorial service, I received a phone call from David, Jeff's younger brother. "I will be in Madison sometime next week, and I thought I'd like to come by and visit with you," he said.

"That would be wonderful," I responded, but the next week came and went, and I never heard back from him. Since his identity is a secret, I had no way of contacting him. I was sad. I would have liked to talk with him.

I continued receiving letters from Jeff's girlfriends, but gradually those stopped coming. One woman remained in contact for a few years, but eventually, that ended too.

A movie producer contacted me about making a movie about Jeff from a Christian perspective. I had her contact Lionel, who seemed enthusiastic about the project, but his wife, Shari, was not interested. She felt it was exploitative and wanted nothing to do with it. The project died, never getting funding to proceed.

From time to time someone remembers my association with Jeffrey Dahmer, but for the most part, my life has returned to normal. Because of Jeff, I have become involved in prison ministry. Now, I am visiting five prisoners in five different prisons. It is strange that I had never been to a prison before knowing Jeffrey Dahmer. Now, that work occupies much of my time.

Jeffrey Dahmer changed my life. My present prison ministry is an ongoing memorial to him, and my entire ministry is an ongoing memorial to Jesus Christ. Jeff simply illustrates what Jesus can do with sinful men.

CHAPTER 14
REFLECTIONS: SANE OR INSANE?

"Dahmer pleaded guilty but insane before the trial.

The psychiatric experts who would testify also agreed

that he knew right from wrong. This left just two questions

for Dahmer's jury to decide: Did he have a mental disease

and, if so, could he have controlled his conduct

and chosen to stop killing?"

JOAN ULLMAN

PSYCHOLOGY TODAY, MAY 1992

I AM often asked if I think Jeff was sane or insane.

The question carries with it the most intense emotions. I think people want me to say that Jeff was insane so they can deal more easily with the heinousness and bizarre aspects of his crimes. Some people want to think Jeff was insane, not evil, so his crimes can be explained and accepted. Others simply believe he was evil.

A number of psychiatrists studied Jeff and found him to be sane. But this doesn't satisfy many questioners. It is nearly impossible to think of the horrible acts he committed and connect that with a sane man. How could anyone do what he did and still be sane? Don't the acts themselves prove his insanity?

I never considered Jeff insane. The dictionary defines insanity as being of unsound mind and being mentally deranged. Derangement is defined as "being disordered and disarranged." In other words, an insane man is one who is "out of his head" or "not in his right mind," mentally out of order and distressed. This feeling causes him to behave in strange ways that are not appropriate.

Once I heard a Christian psychologist describe insanity with this story. "Imagine a man comes into church one Sunday with a bag full of hamburgers he's bought at a fast-food restaurant. As he walks down the aisle, he approaches people with a hamburger in hand and tries to give the food away. He becomes forceful, saying, 'What's the matter? You have to eat! Take it!' The man is concerned about a human need, but has lost his sense of the appropriate. Trying to force people to eat hamburgers during a church service is inappropriate. The man doesn't understand the proper order of things. He is insane."

The insane man has not lost his ability to speak his language or dress himself or even accomplish some tasks, but his focus has shifted. He is bothered by things most people consider unimportant.

Once I asked another psychologist to describe sanity. She said the definition differs with the way you view it. Sanity can be viewed in a philosophical way, a clinical way and a legal way.

The legal definition is the easiest to deal with. Two things define insanity in the courts: first, that a defendant was unable to determine right from wrong at the time of the crime, and second, that the defendant was unable to appreciate the consequences of his actions at the time of the crime.

Based on this legal definition, Jeff was sane. He demonstrated by his actions that he knew the difference between right and wrong. He showed that he understood the consequences of his actions by hiding his crimes and lying to police officers. He knew his acts would get him into trouble, so he hid what he was doing.

The clinical definition of insanity is more difficult. It involves the meaning of "mental disorder." Mental disorders have specific criteria for diagnosis. Insanity is not a mental disorder. Mental disorders are more specific—depression, anxiety, psychosis. Insanity is simply too big a word to fit into these kinds of definitions.

Mental disorders are significant behavioral or psychological syndromes or patterns that occur in an individual and are associated with present distress or disability or with a significantly increased risk of death, pain, disability or a loss of freedom. A person demonstrating deviant behavior doesn't have a mental disorder unless the behavior is a symptom of a dysfunction in the individual. In other words, although Jeff's crimes were horribly deviant, they were not fueled by a mental disorder.

Jeff did suffer from necrophilia, and many people would classify that as a psychological dysfunction, but it did not reveal itself in his normal behavior. It was something he fought within himself, and only came to the surface when he finally gave in to his evil urges.

The clearest way to be determined legally insane is to demonstrate a psychosis. People with psychoses are out of touch with reality. They see things that others don't, hear things others don't and sometimes even smell things others don't. To them, their reality is as real as any object you or I would examine. They have delusions—that is, ideas in their heads that are out of touch with reality, but seem completely real to them. The authorities who examined Jeff concluded that he wasn't suffering from a psychosis.

Thus, when asked, I usually say I don't believe Jeffrey Dahmer was insane. I never saw anything in him to indicate to me that he was off track mentally. As far as I could tell, Jeff was as sane as anyone.

Over the years in my ministry, I have had to deal with all kinds of people.

Many of them have had serious problems. Some have acted in bizarre and unusual ways. One person in my office began complimenting me about something, and the very next moment began screaming at me for some slight I supposedly committed. Another person I dealt with was calm and lucid, but suddenly began telling me about hearing voices and of conspiracies in the making. These people were not "in their right minds."

On the other hand, I have sat with people who were so emotionally distraught they could not make any decision without asking for my opinion, advice, or preferably my decision on how they should decide. I have been there when people experienced the death of a loved one, when they suffered disappointments and losses and when they were told of their own coming death. I have seen people in nearly every emotional circumstance imaginable. None of these people would be classified as insane. All of them had profound problems that were not easily addressed, much less solved. Yet none of them was as composed emotionally and mentally as Jeff was with me. He came across as normal.

Once, while we were studying the book of Hebrews, I made the point that sin will destroy you, and that there is a deceitfulness to sin.

Jeff's comments, I think, demonstrate his sanity. He said, "I can relate to that. When I was committing my crimes, I felt that as long as I could hide them away so no one could see what I'd done, I wouldn't have to deal with my crimes or think about them. I could go about acting like a normal person, and feel like a normal person."

Isn't that like all of us? As long as we can hide our bruises with long sleeves, no one has to know about the beatings. If no one can see the needle marks, no one will know about our drug habit. When no one sees the tears, no one will know of our heartache or our problem. We can go to church, go to the store, go to work and interact with other people as if nothing had ever happened. If we never talk about the sexual abuse at home, our children can act like normal children at school. As long as we cover up our crimes, we can pretend they never happened. That's what Jeff did.

The psychologist I referred to earlier told me an interesting anecdote about the sanity question. She said, "In a class in graduate school, one of my professors gave us a test profile and some background of an anonymous person and asked us to determine if this person was sane, that is, able to tell right from wrong and able to appreciate the consequences of his actions. It was an interesting exercise, and we all agreed that the person probably was sane. Then she gave us the punch line—the test profile was of Jeffrey Dahmer."

There you have it. The authorities concluded that Jeffrey Dahmer was sane.

But this conclusion brings with it cause for concern. The ramifications trouble us. If Jeff could do what he did and still be sane, what about the rest of us? Are we all capable of such heinous crimes ourselves? Could we do what Jeff did? I think the answer is yes.

Jeff was a sinner. His life proves there is no limit to our capacity to sin or be cruel to other people. We are all candidates for murder and mayhem. It doesn't take crazy people to do such things.

What it does take is a total disregard for other people. I think it is faith in God that makes us care about others. When God is ignored, and we live our lives as if He doesn't exist, there is a profound effect on our actions and psyche. This is not to say that all atheists become murderers, but it is to say that not believing in God allows us to justify the most evil treatment of other people. Jeff's faith in God changed his perception of people.

This all suggests something frightening—that any of us could become monsters. I believe any of us are capable of everything Jeff did, if we leave God out of our lives. Jeff's life declares the message that believing in God is a necessity. We must live for Him.

Dr. Lauren Cunningham, psychologist, Madison, Wisconsin, consulted on this chapter.

CHAPTER 15
REFLECTIONS: WAS HE SINCERE?

"I just want to say that I hope that God has forgiven

me. I think He has. I know society will never be able to forgive

me for what I have done. But if there is a God in heaven, I promise

I will pray each day to ask them [the families] for their forgiveness."

JEFFREY DAHMER'S STATEMENT TO THE COURT, 1992

ONE of the most common questions put to me about Jeff has to do with the sincerity of his faith. And I usually hear this from Christians. They ask if Jeff was truly sincere in his desire for baptism and in his Christian life. My answer is always the same: Yes, I am convinced he was sincere.

This question bothers me. Why question the sincerity of another person's faith? Baptism represents a change in lifestyle. A person is expected to change after being baptized. When people don't change, we begin to wonder. Why were they baptized? Did they did not really comprehend what was involved?

I can understand those kinds of questions.

But Jeff's circumstance was different. The people asking me didn't know about his post-baptismal life. They were basing their question on what he did before he was baptized, not after. That bothers me.

Jeff was judged not by his faith, but by his crimes. The questioner always seemed to hope I'd answer: "No, he wasn't sincere." The questioner seemed to be looking for a way to reject Jeffrey as a brother in Christ instead of seeing him as a sinner who has come to God. The subtext of such questions was simple. They didn't want to think of Jeff as a brother. Such ungraciousness is contrary to the Christian spirit.

Was Jeff saved? Were his sins taken away? Was he a Christian believer? Did he repent of his sins? Or was the blood of Christ shed on the cross somehow too weak, too thin, and too anemic to cover his sins? Did Jeff mean it when he said, "I'm so sorry for what I've done. God help me, I'll never do that again"?

Why was it inconceivable that Jeffrey Dahmer could come to faith?

I became convinced of Jeff's sincerity by one happening. On a certain visit we came to the end of our study time together. The prison guard had given us the signal, but right then, before I stood to leave, Jeff bared his soul.

"I feel very, very bad about the crimes I've committed. In fact, I think I should have been put to death by the state for what I did."

"I agree with you," I said. "You should have been put to death by the state for the crimes you committed."

He replied, "If that is true, am I sinning against God by continuing to live?"

"Boy, you sure picked a time to bring this up," I answered. "We can't go into all this now, but I can see where you are going." I asked him to read the first half of Romans 13 (13:1-7) before my next visit. "That passage relates to your question," I said.

"I will. Take care—I'll see you next time," he said as I left.

On the drive home all this ran through my mind. Jeff was thinking of suicide. Would he take matters into his own hands and kill himself? Did he feel so bad about himself that he no longer wanted to live?

The subject of suicide goes deep into my soul. Once in my life I contemplated suicide. I was fired from my position of many years as minister of a church in Northern Wisconsin. The area was relatively remote, and the church was unable to find a replacement. When I couldn't find another position in another church, we reached a compromise. I would continue as minister for another eight months, after which time we would part company.

As a minister and a preacher, I was a failure. Every time I went to church and faced my congregation, that message came through. My self-confidence and self-esteem eroded. I began to believe the church's opinion of me. Had I wasted my life as a minister? The ministry was the only thing I knew; it was the basis of my identity.

I began to lose interest in my work, and my conviction grew that my life had no meaning. I wanted to escape, but there was no place to run. Increasingly, the only option that had any appeal was death. I wanted to escape this human experience. Even facing an angry God was preferable to this.

Finally, it was Susan, my wife, who brought me out of my despair. I mentioned to her once, "I think things would be better if I were dead." She shrugged off my words and said, "Don't be silly." She responded the same way the second time I brought it up and the third time, too. After the fourth or fifth time, she stopped and looked at me long and hard.

"You really mean this, don't you?" she asked. I nodded my head and said nothing. I was driving the car at the time. She began to weep hysterically. She was inconsolable. Her reaction took me by surprise; I didn't expect her to cry.

"How could you think such a thing?" she said between gasps. "What will happen to us?"

"What do you mean?" I responded.

"If you are gone, where will we live? Who will take care of us? What are we supposed to do without you?" she cried.

In my deep depression, I hadn't even considered the effect my suicide would have on Susan, my son, my daughter, much less my parents, my siblings and others who mattered to me. I hadn't even thought about that. I was so consumed with my feelings that I hadn't thought about anyone else. I was not in my right mind. I was not insane, but I was not rational either.

"You're so right. I'm so sorry. I'll stop this," I told her and dried her tears. Susan had delivered me.

At my next meeting with Jeff, I began with his question, "Am I sinning against God by continuing to live?"

I told him, "Romans 13 does say God has placed a sword in the hand of the governing authority. That's why I agreed with you last week when you said you thought the state should have put you to death."

"Yes," he replied. "But has the state failed its duty by not putting me to death?"

"I can't answer that question. I can say that God has put a sword in the state's hand, and the state has that right from God. This state has apparently chosen to lay down its sword and take up a rod instead.

"What is our responsibility to the state?" I asked him.

"Well, Scripture says the Christian must submit to the governing authority," Jeff replied.

"Right. We aren't to judge the state for what the state has decided to do, but submit to the state. By continuing to live, you are submitting to the state."

"I see," he said, thinking about what I had said.

"What that means is that you must try to be the best prisoner you can be. You must not disobey the rules, nor subvert the system. You accept your position as a prisoner of the state for life, and serve God as best as you can for as long as God allows you to live."

"Okay," was all he said.

But I wasn't finished with him yet. "When you ask, 'Am I sinning by continuing to live?' are you implying that you are thinking of suicide?" I pressed.

"Yes, I admit I've thought of suicide."

"Well, I'm going to make a confession to you. I have thought of it, too," I told him. "There was a time in my life when I couldn't bear the thought of living any longer. I wanted to die."

"Me too. But when I thought I should take my life, I just couldn't do it," he confessed.

I confessed my experience as well. "When I came to myself, I realized I hadn't been thinking right. I had no concern for others, for my wife or my children. All I thought about was myself. Suicide is a selfish thing."

Jeff listened intently to what I said. "My main concern is that I do the right thing," he replied.

After that, how could I question Jeff's sincerity? Jeff wanted to please God. He knew he had done terrible things, and he needed me to tell him that his life mattered regardless. I could relate to how he felt. I understood his heart.

After this discussion, I begin to revisit what had brought me to the point of suicide. I was able to reframe what had happened to me as God's workings in my life. What had happened prepared me to help Jeff.

I had already studied the religious issues that perplexed Jeff, and I had resolved them in my mind. I had faced suicide, and I could help Jeff think differently about that, too. God had prepared me to minister to his needs. God, in His Providence, shaped and molded me to meet the needs of a young man He knew was going to be in trouble. He brought me to Madison against my will. I would have never left that northern Wisconsin church on my own, and I left there with bitterness in my heart and anger toward God. Realizing all this helped me put my bitterness away. I no longer blamed God for what had happened to me. I finally forgave those who hurt me years ago. They were doing God's work without realizing it. They were part of God's Providence.

EPILOGUE
I CALLED HIM JEFF

"This is my first effort at writing, and I was reluctant to do it,

not because I didn't want to tell the story, but because

I didn't think people would be interested. But several people

have badgered me over the years, so I wrote it. My focus was to show

that there were three stories here: Jeff's story, my story and God's

story. I wanted to show that God was at work in both my

story and Jeff's story to bring us together and to

bring about his salvation."

LETTER FROM ROY RATCLIFF, 2005

ROB McRay called me shortly after Jeff's memorial service to arrange a time to interview me. He had written an article about Jeff's baptism for the Christian magazine *Wineskins,* and now wanted to write another about my friendship with Jeff. Rob has felt close to the story since he was the one who called me originally about baptizing Jeff. We set up December 26, 1994, the day after Christmas, for the interview.

Rob began, "Like I've told you, I had a hard time at first telling the story of Jeff's conversion and writing the article I wrote for *Wineskins.* I've had a hard time moving from calling him Dahmer to calling him Jeffrey. In Milwaukee, it was Dahmer, Dahmer, Dahmer—that's what we all called him. But as I began to think of him in terms of your studies with him and his conversion, I began to work on calling him Jeffrey. It didn't seem right to call someone that you're trying to teach 'Dahmer.' But I noticed that you call him Jeff, and I'm interested in that. Was that a request of his? Why did you call him that?"

"It came naturally from knowing him," I said. "He wasn't just Dahmer to me. Calling a person by his last name is alienating and distancing. It reminds me of being in physical education class in high school where I was only known as Ratcliff. It's a good way to distance yourself from another person to avoid getting to know them."

"Each week, Jeff and I sat down across from each other at a table. We would shake hands. I would show him my Bible. He could read right out of my Bible, and I could read out of his," I explained. "I could point out different things from our different translations. We were able to connect person-to-person."

"He became a real person to me. In one way, I was blessed, as I had a certain ignorance of all the gory details of his crimes, so I didn't have that to inhibit me. Later, at the insistence of Susan, I did read various books about Jeff's crimes. I was deeply shaken by the details. But that did not alter the connection I had made with him as a person. He became a real person to me, so I referred to him the same way I would anyone I knew personally."

Since that interview, I've contemplated Rob's point, and I find myself more firmly established in my position. I challenge others who refer to Jeff by his last name. Usually, those who write me begin by proclaiming their Christian faith and praising me for my role in Jeff's story, and then they ask me about Jeff—using only his last name. I respond by asking, "If he is a brother in Christ, why not speak of him with the same familiarity we use for others?"

The greatest thing I learned from Jeff is that he was a person with needs, just like the rest of us. He was just as disturbed about his crimes as everyone else. He had fears and concerns and dreams and hopes as we all do. He was a person, not a monster. He needed God, and when he found God, his life was enriched and blessed.

I am a better man for knowing him. I didn't see this at first. After Jeff was murdered, and television and radio reporters interviewed me, they often asked, "How has this experience changed your life?"

My answer was that it hadn't changed my life. I was still too close to the experience. I needed time to reflect on the changes in me because Jeff was interposed into my life. Now that more than ten years have passed, I can look back and see the effects more clearly.

The way I value human life has changed. A quotation of Jeff's from his Dateline NBC interview often comes to mind. How did he feel while committing his crimes? "I felt that I didn't have to be accountable to anyone," he said. "Since man came from slime, I was accountable to no one."

His words have a certain logic. If human beings are nothing more than refined slime or complicated amoeba, then killing other creatures, especially those less complicated or clever than you, is justifiable. But once you accept the reality that humans are specially created in the image of God, the value of human life changes. Once Jeff embraced his faith in God, his view of humanity changed. He began to value human life and recognized his responsibility to protect, not destroy it.

As I think my way through Jeff's changing value system, I find that I too have devalued human life. I have never killed another human being, but I have certainly thought badly of others. Knowing Jeff has taught me to listen to Jesus' teaching in the Sermon on the Mount. Jesus speaks out against murder, but focuses more on our anger toward others. God values people. So should we.

I've also learned that great harm comes when we disconnect from other people. In his early life, Jeff disconnected from his fellow human beings. When we choose to depersonalize someone—whether Jeff, by using his last name or making him the object of jokes, or someone else—we are starting down the road of disconnecting.

It seems a strange thing to say, but I think I've seen viciousness and cold-bloodedness from those who talk about Jeff that rivals the viciousness of his crimes. I've heard of Christian people saying, "If Dahmer goes to heaven, I don't want to go there." How foolish. Our God is a forgiving God—that's His business. Are human beings worthy of Christ's death? No, but he died for us anyway.

Because of Jeff, I value church life more deeply. The church has always been a basic element in my experience, but I've seen the other side of the tracks through Jeff. With no foundation of faith, how can families cope with the great difficulties of life? I believe profound things happen to children when they see adult role models expressing faith in God. Jeff's father had faith in God, but when problems arose at home, Lionel quit taking Jeff and abandoned the church. I have often wondered if someone or something could've helped Jeff—if his father had taken him to church. The value of church life has become more precious to me.

The emotional distance between father and son in this tragedy is profound. My heart goes out to Lionel in his efforts to reach out to his sons after years of emotional distance. It is easy, when there are serious problems between husband and wife—as was the case with Jeff's parents—to shut off the children as well. In marital wars, children are usually the greatest casualties.

Jeff and I talked a lot about his parents. He loved them both. He grieved over their wars. After being divorced for many years, their relationship was as bitter and harsh as the day they parted. Most of the prayers we prayed were on his parents' behalf. Whether his family's turmoil gave birth to his crimes is unknowable. But it is significant to me that Jeff's first murder took place the summer he was abandoned by both mother and father.

Jeff fostered in me greater compassion and understanding for those imprisoned. I now work with prisoners in several prisons. Some of them openly confess that they are guilty and deserve what they are getting. Because of Jeff, I can look into their souls and see real people.

Several years ago, I was working at Fallhall Glen, my Christian camp, with a group of 13- to 15-year-olds. At that time, Court TV was producing a documentary on Jeff and insisted on interviewing me at the camp. Bringing in a television camera crew introduced Jeff's story to our campers, who were generally unaware of my involvement with him. After the interview ended and the camera crew left, we talked with these young teens about the forgiveness of sins.

A few days later, I had to call a boy—a wrongdoer on a downhill path— to my office. I gave him a punishment that would last until camp was over, but my heart went out to him. I talked to him about the place of God in our lives. When I looked into his eyes, I was thinking of a young Jeffrey. What if someone had sat and talked with him about God and faith when he was this age? Could it have made a difference in some way?

All in all, I want the world to know that I called him Jeff. He was my friend and my brother in faith. I look forward to seeing him in heaven, for his sins are washed away. God snatched him from the fires of hell. Jesus came and died and rose again for him.

Jeff's story is a powerful one of a transformed life, but it is more than that. It shows how far God can reach to save a soul. It shows what God may do in the life of a person like me to prepare him for God's work. A younger version of me could not have dealt with Jeffrey Dahmer. God was working in my life for His purposes. Jeff's story is the story of a God who works in this world.

In Psalm 8 in the Old Testament, David views the heavens at night, looks at the stars and glories in the majesty of God. He asks, "What is man that you are mindful of him?" We are so insignificant and unimportant in the grand scheme of things. Why does God care? Given His greatness, His care is overwhelming. It matters when we fall and when we cry and when we need Him. God loves us all, no matter how badly we have messed up our lives. If God can love Jeffrey Dahmer, he can love you and me, too.

I hope and pray that Jeff's story and my story will be a testament that helps you see the story God is writing for your life. In the end, that is all that matters.

BIBLIOGRAPHY

A Father's Story, by Lionel Dahmer, William Morrow and Company, New York, 1994. Lionel Dahmer's haunting first-person account of his life with his son. Lionel Dahmer holds a Ph.D. in chemistry and worked as a chemist for many years.

"I carried it too far, that's for sure," Joan Ullman, *Psychology Today*, May 1992. Reflections, especially regarding aspects of the insanity defense, by a journalist who observed the Dahmer trial.

"Inside Evil: Jeffrey Dahmer," *Dateline NBC*, November 29, 1994. An interview of Jeffrey Dahmer by Stone Phillips. The program aired the day after Dahmer's death.

"Jeffrey Dahmer, The Monster Within," The Biography Channel. A chronological account of Jeffrey Dahmer's life. For a summary transcript see www.thebiography-channel.co.uk.

"The Chief of Sinners," by Rob McRay, *Wineskins Magazine*, Vol. 2, No. 6, 1994. An account by Rob McRay, the minister who asked Roy Ratcliff to baptize Jeffrey Dahmer, about grappling with the issues of grace in Dahmer's story.

"The Life and Crimes of Jeffrey Dahmer," *Crime Stories*, CourtTV. An account similar to that produced by The Biography Channel. Includes discussions of Dahmer by psychiatrists who studied him.

The Man Who Could Not Kill Enough, by Anne E. Schwartz, Birch Lane Press, New York, 1992. One of many graphic accounts of the horrors of Jeffrey Dahmer's murders. Schwartz, a *Milwaukee Journal* crime reporter, broke the story in the press. The book begins with Dahmer's arrest and ends with the conclusion of his trial.

Step into My Parlor: The Chilling Story of Serial Killer Jeffrey Dahmer, by Ed Baumann, Bonus Books, Inc., Chicago, 1991. Another of the graphic accounts of Jeffrey Dahmer's crimes. It is quoted in Chapter 3 of this book. Baumann's account begins shortly before Dahmer's arrest and ends when he is charged with the murders.

Note

1. Ed Bauman, *Step into My Parlor: The Chilling Story of Serial Killer Jeffrey Dahmer* (Chicago, IL: Bonus Books, 1991).